GRIZZLY's
This 'N That

by

Ray Racobs

authorHOUSE°

AuthorHouse™
1663 Liberty Drive
Bloomington, IN 47403
www.authorhouse.com
Phone: 1 (800) 839-8640

Published by AuthorHouse 04/18/2017

ISBN: 978-1-4184-6922-1 (sc)

Library of Congress Control Number: 2004098831

Print information available on the last page.

Grizzly's This 'N That

By

Ray "Grizzly" Racobs

Illustrations by Monica Frey

Dedicated to Lynda,

my lovely and wonderful wife,

who has been the best part of my life.

GRIZZLY'S THIS 'N THAT

TABLE OF CONTENTS

GRIZZLY'S THIS 'N THAT

TABLE OF ILLUSTRATIONS

Don't cry over spilt milk.

IN THE BEGINNING

    For the past five years, I have substituted for teachers in three area school districts. I was filling in for a sick third grade teacher when I had occasion to repeat an old saying to one of the students. A shy little girl in the class had knocked her box of colored pencils and crayons off her desk. She began to cry. I approached her, told her it was all right, and said, "There's no need to cry over spilt milk." The young girl immediately quit crying, looked up at me, and said, "Mr. Racobs, I didn't spill my milk."

    For some reason one evening, soon after the incident, I began writing down all the sayings and proverbs that came to mind. I added to the list, off and on, for some time and the collection grew. I began to ask family members, friends, and others what their favorite sayings or quotes were. Every now and then, someone would mention one that I had forgotten about or hadn't even heard before.

My little writing journal began to fill up. My wife, Lynda, mentioned that I should organize the entries and have it published. Lynda, who teaches fourth grade, had written and illustrated a children's book about Cricket, her sheltie. She was in the process of getting her book professionally printed. I figured we may as well both be "published".

Many sayings, proverbs, and quotes often triggered recollections in my mind about my own experiences and stories from my past. I began to incorporate them into the book. This was when I actually came up with the title, *Grizzly's This 'N That.* For many months in my spare time I typed. I arranged, added, deleted, rearranged, added, deleted, and rearranged some more. I was about edited out, but finally finished my little piece of literary work.

I wanted to break up the anecdotes, sayings and quotes with a little more variety and humor. I came up with "Grizzly's definitions" for various words and added them (or threw them in, if you prefer) throughout the book. They are not totally serious, but they are true and appropriate, as I see it. I feel there are many lessons to be learned in most of the subjects covered and I hope you will be enjoy reading it.

Great minds think alike.

FIRST THINGS FIRST

All right, ***first things first***, which, by the way, is the first of many sayings, proverbs or quotes that I have included in the book. The text is meant to be informative as well as humorous in nature. Most of the sayings and proverbs have been around for many centuries, but that doesn't mean they are out of date. They have withstood the test of time and their use, with a few exceptions, should be continued.

If many of us would include an occasional old saying or proverb appropriately in our conversation and writings, we might very well be viewed by others as more interesting and intelligent. Our lives and our interactions with others, may well, or at least should, improve if we incorporated the positive points of many of the old sayings into how we live and act.

The selected sayings or quotes are reproduced in bold print. The bracketed [.....] text denotes where I have taken the liberty to add to or modify any of the sayings presented. My intention for changing any selection was two fold. I wanted to add more humor to the book, for the reader, and secondly, I wanted it to be more enjoyable to write.

Most of the proverb books I have seen will repeat any given entry several times throughout the book. The simple saying, ***a dog is a man's best friend,*** is often repeated after the alphabetized headings for "dog", "man", "best", and "friend". Now to me, that is being just a little too redundant. I have, for the most part, not done this, because *Grizzly's This 'N That* is not meant to be a boring book for research, but a book to be enjoyed.

Some of my stories may not pertain directly to the chapter headings where they are presented, but the saying brought up the memory. After all it is my book.

By the way, some of the wording of the sayings may not be what you recall them to be. I will explain. I have written the sayings or quotes as I have remembered them or as I have heard them from others. I could have taken them directly from any of a variety of proverb books, but chose not to.

*

All work and no play makes Jack a dull boy.

WHO IS GRIZZLY?

The staff and girls who attend Girl Scout camps in the summer, choose "camp names" to go by, instead of their real names. I do not know why, unless it's to make camp more fun.

For twenty camp seasons, as the Ranger at Camp Seikooc my camp name was "Dudley". I chose it back in 1980, in memory of my favorite uncle. I lived and worked on the camp year around. I had every intention of retiring at Seikooc, but that was not to be, since the Girl Scouts sold the property. Although I didn't retire there, Dudley did.

I transferred to Starwood's Outdoor Center early in 2000. I chose "Grizzly" as my new camp name and selected it for several reasons.

1. One of the creatures I have respected is the bear. In Colorado there are presumably no Grizzlies, but I admire them just the same.

2. I obtained my associates degree from Butler County Community College. Their mascot is the grizzly.

3. The Girl Scout Camp Wiedemann Ranger's camp name is "Bear" and his son is "Little Bear".

4. Grizzlies are one of the largest bears found in the U.S. At 6'4" and 220 pounds, I am not a small guy.

5. "Grizzly" just seemed to suit me, for I look a little grizzled.

I have had Grizzly as a camp name now for over three years and I like being called Grizzly. I can always count on some bear related stuff as gifts from those who know anything about me.

Around Wichita, "bear things" are available for sale, but grizzly bear items are very hard to find. A grizzly bear in the wild in Colorado would be very rare, if present at all, but one can find plenty of items there with a grizzly bear theme.

Incidentally, Lynda's camp name is "Coyote" and it is ironic, but in Wichita you can find a lot of coyote stuff, but not in Colorado, where the wolf seems to dominate. Now if you travel down to New Mexico or Arizona it is a different story. Lynda has directed day camp and held other camp positions over the years. She was a troop leader for her girls and led them from Brownies through the Senior level of Girl Scouting.

Fox in charge of the chicken coop.

ANIMALS IN GENERAL

A number of years ago, I was licensed with the state as a wildlife rehabilitator. It was a very interesting and rewarding experience. I had the opportunity to take care of many wonderful creatures.

I would get calls from various sources about injured or abandoned animals in need of care. The position was an unpaid, volunteer service, so I was not forced to take on all animals, but I never turned any requests down. I once drove about 50 miles to retrieve a robin that had been mauled by a cat. The bird died before I made it back home. The ideal scenario was to care for an animal until it could be released back to nature.

Lynda really enjoyed assisting me in the care and I often needed the help. There were successes, but most stories had unhappy endings. We cared for hawks, owls, and other birds, animals, and reptiles.

I received a call one Monday morning on a hot summer day. I was asked to meet the foreman of a construction company east of town. He showed me to a portable metal storage building. Inside was an adult female fox. She had evidently entered the box the previous Friday and gotten locked in when the workers left for the weekend. I very cautiously approached the fox, but she made no effort to move. The heat had taken its toll on her. I picked her up and took her home.

It was like taking care of a newborn animal, because she could not drink or eat on her own. After several days of care she finally was able to stand and walk around. Sly, as we named her, did get better, but she just didn't seem right. We soon realized that she had no hearing. A week later Sly had gone blind. She knew of our presence and where her food was, due to her sense of smell. Unfortunately, a few days later even that disappeared. The heat exposure had been too much for her to function and after a month we lost her. Lynda was very upset over Sly's demise. As for me.....it was one of the saddest moments in my life.

I made a little casket and put the following inscription on it: "Sly, we did not know you very long, but Lynda and I loved you deeply." I cried the whole time I was working on the box. In fact, I am teary eyed as I make this entry. We buried Sly in the camp's arboretum.

Lynda and I have two favorite stories of success from our rehab experiences. We acquired three orphaned, newborn raccoons. We bottle fed them goat's milk and were helped with the feeding program by our cat, who opportunely had a litter of kittens. She accepted the weird strangers without complaint. Two of the three infant raccoons did not live long, but the third, "Slim", happily did well and progressed admirably. He was an enjoyable addition to the household. Slim enjoyed playing with Cricket, our sheltie, but for some reason didn't like being with the kittens he had been reared with.

We kept him in the house, as if he were a puppy, until he became old enough to be transferred to the barn. As he grew he would enjoy playing with us and our full grown black lab. Lynda made him a cozy little home out among the hay bales. Then one day he didn't seem to be around.

As it turned out, he had suddenly become nocturnal, as was his destiny. Lynda and I would go to the barn, in the late evening, to put out food for him. If we called him by name he would scurry out of the stack of hay to greet us and gratefully accept our offerings. He hung around all that first winter, but he left in the spring, we assumed, to start his own life as a creature of the wild.

The second most enjoyable success story involved a young doe. I obtained her from another rehabilitator, who didn't have room to continue her care. She was still weak and sickly after being swept away by a flash flood. We named her Ginny. She responded well to our care. Later we decided to turn her loose on the property, which consisted of 160 acres of open area, tall grass, and timber. The land was fenced with seven-foot tall chain link, which would keep her in until she grew and matured.

Lynda and I set up a feeding station for Ginny near an interior road by a group of trees. I would visit the site with regularity to drop off grain for her. I could call for her and if she was close by she would show up and eat out of my hand. One fine day, she walked out of the tall grass with her first fawn. It was so rewarding to know that I had been a part of bringing that little one into the world.

Lynda and I lived at the camp for another two years, before the Girl Scouts sold the property. We left Ginny behind to the home that she knew. Before we moved, Ginny had given birth to other young. On one such occasion, she had twins. Her fawns never would come up to us like Ginny did, but that was all right. It was such a pleasure to be in their presence just the same.

*

If you mess with the bull you will get the horn
*

If you run after two hares, you will catch neither
*

Don't let the fox be in charge of the chicken coop
*

"I like pigs. Dogs look up at us. Cats look down on us. Pigs treat us as equals."
Sir Winston Churchill
*

Most of us have not been too comfortable, at one time or another, in our job or position. We have been like a…..

Fish out of water
*

I would like to include some information on my new favorite animal of the wild, which of course is the bear. The information could keep you out of trouble in case you run into the awkward situation of meeting a bear face to face. If you never get out to bear country, I am sorry, for you have missed some of the most beautiful country in the world.

True, bears have killed humans, but most people were being ***stupid in a no stupid zone.*** Bears would just as soon be on their own, since they are solitary animals by nature, except during the breeding season. In the FYI file, I recall that dogs in the states where bears reside kill far more people. The key word may be "reside", because bears have continually lost their territory to peoples "need" to expand theirs.

Bears have an excellent sense of smell and they have a ravenous appetite. Mix those two factors and you have an animal that will smell out food and go to it. Do you want a bear to visit your campsite? Then by all means, leave your food and trash out at night. It is much more convenient to store your food and trash in your vehicle, but NOT in your tent. If you are backpacking hang your food up in the air.

Lynda and I were tent camping at the Mizpa Campground in the Arapaho National Forest when an eye opening event occurred. It was in the wee hours of the morning when there arose such a clatter....this sounds familiar....anyway.....We were quite rudely awakened by a loud banging. At first I thought a car

17

door was being opened and slammed shut. I slowly began to come to my senses from such a sound sleep. I realized that it had to be a bear trying to get into the dumpster out near the road.

It was only about thirty feet from our camp. We were both wide awake now and quietly went over our choices, which were few. We could sit it out in the tent or leave the tent and make a dash for the Jeep. Later, you will run across *"When in doubt, do nothing"* and that is what we did. It was only partial relief to us that the noise outside quit. The bear may have given up on the trash dumpster, but may have decided to inspect our tent. Fortunately, the local resident went somewhere else in search of food.

If I slept any more that early morning it must not have been for long. At daybreak, we went out to the dumpster to look around. There were muddy bear prints on all four sides of it. The large dumpster had been moved a foot from where it had been, so it had been no small bear. I could not move the container by myself. When we have pitched a tent since then I do not pick a site close to a dumpster.

I carry a .38 caliber pistol with me when we hike in the mountains. It is for protection from crazy humans, not wild animals. I have heard horror stories about bad things happening to some unsuspecting or vulnerable hikers. I had the weapon that night, but thankful that the use of it was not necessary.

On the trail, in bear country, it is always a good idea to make some kind of noise. Bears will normally avoid humans whenever possible. I have a good-sized Christmas bell on my walking stick, but I do get tired of the noise myself.

If precautions happen to fail, and you should meet a bear, try not to panic. Running off may work, but no one can outrun a bear. If it is a black bear one can usually make loud noises and retreat slowly. If the bear should happen to be a grizzly, do not make noises, but do retreat slowly and quietly. Don't be confused with the name "black" bear. Some black bears are brown in color. Grizzlies are much bigger and have the distinctive hump on their shoulders. It is actually a bundle of muscle.

I would suggest you do some research on what wild animals may be present in the area of your hike and plan ahead of time what actions or non-actions you will take. I have run across only one black bear face to face, while hiking in the wild, and he (or she) took off as soon as our eyes met, but it certainly sent chills up my spine.

I have retrieved some information on the web that gives hikers some advice, if physically attacked by a bear. If it is a black bear fight back in any way possible. If it is a grizzly bear, "play dead". If a grizzly senses you are no threat, hopefully, he will cease the aggression. I would have a hard time lying there while a grizzly chewed on me.

*

Bird in the hand.

ANIMALS – BIRDS

The owl is the king of the night
*

If it looks like a duck, walks like a duck, and talks like a duck, it must be a duck

That one was a favorite of my former District Fire Chief Bill Walker. He told us if we didn't look like firefighters, the public would never respect us as firefighters. When he first came to Andover from Hutchinson, Kansas, the department had only one full time firefighter. The other thirty were all volunteers and it was a fairly untrained, rag tag outfit. The crew didn't "look" very much like firefighters.

Before long, the department had the support from the citizens of the district, a new fire station, new equipment, and a new attitude. By the time Chief Walker left for another fire department, he had turned us into professionals. The city and district had gained better fire protection for their citizens with three shifts of three firefighters on duty for twenty-four hour coverage.

Don't count your chickens before they hatch

Don't put all of your eggs in one basket
*

Lynda had asked me to get her a Rhode Island Red rooster. I gave in one day and the rooster was actually fun to have around. "Red" was afraid of nothing and our dogs left him alone. At least he didn't crow at three o'clock in the morning like some others that I have had. I used to raise them from chicks to serve as food for my owls and hawks.

*

A bird in the hand is worth two in the bush

[A bird in the hand is a hand that will need washing]
*

Every bird loves to hear itself sing
*

The early bird catches the worm
*

Have you ever seen a duck fly in the "V" with geese? I never have. It must be because.....

Birds of a feather stick together

While at Camp Seikooc, I became friends with Larry Yarborough, who was a brick layer. He and his wife, Jan, invited me out to their new country home near El Dorado, KS. It was a splendid place that sat on top of a hill and overlooked much of the countryside. He asked me if I wanted to watch his birds fly. I said, "Sure", but I was a little confused.

He raised Birmingham Rollers. They were a species of pigeon and quite unique. The difference between them and a regular 'ole pigeon was how they flew and what they did when they flew. We walked over to a large box on stilts and opened up one end. Out flew about thirty "rollers". The birds flew together as a group about two hundred feet above us. As if on cue, most of the birds seemed to stop in midair and began either fluttering around or actually spinning backwards towards the ground. I had never seen anything like it before and my guess would be that most people haven't either.

I was hooked and just had to have some of them. He was actually overloaded with birds and agreed to give me some. I would have to build a home for the birds, called a "kit box". I could hardly wait and began work on one when I returned home. I modified an old outdoor latrine (privy) that had not been used for years. I drug it out of the tall grass with the camp tractor and set it out in the open field near my house. I built a 4x4x4 box on two sides of the building. It looked like a big "T" when I was done. I could walk inside to feed and water the birds.

Larry gave me thirty birds and wouldn't take any money for them. I was elated. He told me to let them get acclimated to the area before I turned them out to fly. They would not have flown back to his house (they were not homing pigeons), but they would try to find their "home" and probably be lost.

I cared for them for a month, before I set them loose.

In the meantime, Larry got me interested in the Wichita Flying Roller Club. He was one of the officers. The club had monthly competitions with the rollers. Judges would go to each member's house to watch their birds fly. The birds were rated for how well they "kitted" (stayed together in flight) and how well they "spun" or rolled. The quality of a spin was determined with the velocity and duration of the spin.

A person had to fly a minimum of twelve birds. The more birds that spun simultaneously, the more points you earned. I like competition and joined the club.

It takes a lot of work to put together a quality kit of birds to fly in competition, but I had made the commitment and I learned as much as I could about the sport. The results in my first full year of flying my birds shocked most, if not all of the members. My birds took first place overall at the end of the year. I had "dethroned" a veteran in the club, who had monopolized the top spot for years.

I was looking forward to the next season, which began well. I was up near the top in points after three competitions when disaster struck. My bird building was blown over and destroyed from the high winds associated with a tornado that blasted through the area ("Weather" chapter). I had almost 100 birds by then and lost all but ten. I lost my entire competition kit of twenty birds. I also lost my drive and ambition to start over. I miss those crazy birds and may just give Larry another call to see if he might have some spare birds again.

*

Like water off a duck's back
*

A little bird told me
*

Don't let the cat out of the bag.

ANIMALS - CATS

One should have a dog to worship him and a cat to ignore him.

*

A cat is there when you call her, if she doesn't have something better to do.

*

Don't let the cat out of the bag

*

Cats must be smarter than dogs. Have you ever seen eight cats pull a sled through snow

*

Curiosity killed the cat

Cats do, of course, have several lives to spare.

*

"To walk a cat on a leash is against a cats nature."
Adlai Stevenson

*

Has the cat got your tongue?

Long ago, cats were worshipped as god
and they have never forgotten this

*Dogs believe they are human, cats believe they are
god*
*

Time spent with cats is not time wasted
*

*You will always be lucky if you know how to make
friends with strange cats*
*

It is better to feed one cat than many mice

We have three cats that have been freeloaders
for several years now. I believe one of them actually
goes out of his way to search for mice, but the other
two must have retired and are on a pension and I am
the provider. They reside in my workshop, which I
know is not free of mice. That is a good clue that....

Something is not right in Denmark.
*

When winter sets in, we have a mice problem in our house and units around the campsite. I would not mind at all if the "mouser" was given temporary lodging inside the warm confines of our home, just to see if he would help earn his keep, because.....

There should be no free lunch

Lynda, however, has this small hang-up about animal hair on the sofa, etc. I don't see her going out of her way to keep the two "inside" dogs (Cricket and Fletcher) off the furniture, so it seems to be a moot point.

*

To please himself, only the cat purrs
*
If cats could talk, they wouldn't
*
Look what the cat drug in
*

Can't teach an old dog new tricks.

DOGS

Every dog will have his day
*

The fact that I love dogs is evident if you were to visit me, because we have five of them. I honestly feel that five is too many, but only consider two of the dogs living with us as officially mine. I do, however, pay for most of the food and vet bills. At Lynda's request, I bought her a sheltie for her birthday about nine years ago. I was not totally thrilled about the acquisition, since I prefer big dogs, but Cricket has been a remarkably fun dog to own.

Lynda's daughter, Tana, had a dachshund and decided to save money on rent, so moved in with her sister, Kelly. Fletcher's behavior was causing some problems with the living arrangement. Kelly told Tana the dog had to go. He did go..... to our house.

The school nurse, where Lynda teaches, was moving and needed to find a home for their dog Abby, a golden retriever. Somehow, she became a member of the household. I had the impression that Abby was infertile. She may have been, that is, until she hit the ground at our house. Months later, Abby had six puppies, thanks to my neighbor's Great Dane "Casanova", who roams free. In theory, I had no say about the previously mentioned acquisitions. I kept one male puppy from Abby's litter and named him "Oso", which means "bear" in Spanish.

Our fifth canine guest, turned resident, was a walk on. JJ showed up one day, weak and neglected. He appeared to be part greyhound and was so sweet. I just had to keep him. He got his name after helping himself to my coffee, which was sitting on the, where else, coffee table. I first called him Java Joe, but later shortened it.

A dog's lifespan is said to be about one seventh of that for humans. It is a shame that dogs and other pets don't live much longer. I have been the owner or "dad" to many dogs over the years. All my dogs have been great animals. The girls who come to camp have always enjoyed them as well.

Love me, love my dog

*

You can't teach an old dog new tricks
*

MOST IRRITATING NOISE #1

I don't get too bent out of shape when a dog barks for a reason, such as to notify its owner of a possible threat from a cat walking across the lawn. What really bothers me, especially when I am trying to sleep, is when all of the dogs in the area pick up the chant, just because one mutt starts it. What about my dogs, you may ask? They don't, thankfully, bark just because another dog is barking. I can control my dogs, but I can't control those of my neighbors. It is beyond me how any of them can sleep while a Great Dane, a German Shepard, and two labs wail into the night, for whatever reason.

*

The meaning behind this one is along the lines of why someone should do something, like clean house for instance, when they have a maid.

Why keep a dog and bark yourself
*

Let a sleeping dog lie
*

"It is not the size of the dog in the fight; it's the size of the fight in the dog."
Mark Twain

A barking dog never bites

Tell that one to those who deliver your mail and packages or to those who read your electric or water meter.

*

A disclaimer is…..

Three things are not to be trusted; a cow's horn, a dog's tooth, and a horses hoof

*

It's a dog eat dog world out there and I'm wearing Milk Bone underwear

*

Don't bark up the wrong tree

*

You can lead a horse to water…

HORSES

Hold your horses
*

It is too late to close the stable door after the horse has gone
*

A good horse is seldom spurred
*

You can lead a horse to water, but you can't make him drink

Unless the horse is already thirsty
*

That's a horse of a different color
*

    You have, by now viewed a few of the many illustrations in my book. I would be remiss if I didn't mention something about the artist. When I decided to include illustrations in the book, I faced a slight dilemma. I am not at all artistic. I did come up with the illustration about breaking rules, but I was not impressed with the outcome nor the amount of time it took me. I needed to find someone who would do sketches to depict some of the sayings.

I shared my problem with a student, who I had substituted before in art, at the high school. The student said she knew a girl who might be interested. A few days later, I was sitting in for the world history teacher. Each class was to view a rather lengthy and boring movie about the Battle of Waterloo. I had noticed one student in particular who was not only watching the video, but was also taking notes. I guessed she had to be an honor role student. At the end of the period, the attractive young lady came up to me and asked if I knew Sasha. I replied, "Are you the artist?" She was.

Her name is Monica Frey. I briefly detailed what I needed and she said she would take one idea home and draw something up to see what I thought. Monica brought the "lead a horse to water" sketch back to class the next day and I was very pleased

I showed her a few pages of the book and gave her an overview of what my writing project was. I asked Monica to talk it over with her parents. I was extremely pleased and excited when she agreed to do the sketches and be recognized as Grizzly's illustrator. They are, I feel, a nice addition to the book. By the way, I was right. Monica is an "A" student at Clearwater High School.

*

You can't put the cart before the horse

*

Don't change horses in midstream

Don't change them at a gallop either.

*

Every time I ride a horse, wherever the locale may be, I think about the old west and the days when horses were "a man's best friend". I envision myself to be one of the cowboys out on the range. In many ways I wish I had been living during the 1800's, but it would certainly not have been an easy life.

My dad retired from the Air Force in 1961. We moved to the country, south of Salina, KS. We lived in an old, but decent, farm house with a barn, corral, pasture, and the **whole nine yards**. Dad gave my sister and me both a horse. I have loved them ever since. I named mine Cricket. (Coincidently, years later, Lynda actually came up with the same name for her sheltie.)

Cricket was not very well broke, but with a lot of work he became a very good riding horse. The fact amazes me today, because I had next to no previous experience riding horses, much less training them.

Cricket would often lie down beside the barn and bask in the morning sun. My favorite memory of those days was when I went out with a book and laid down beside him, used his neck as a pillow, and read. I should recall that memory more often, since it was a very peaceful and content moment in my life.

A year or so later we moved about forty miles south to another country place. A mile away, *as the crow flies,* lived another family, who farmed. Danny, the oldest boy and I became friends. I was a senior, Danny was a sophomore and he had a sister, Claudia, who was also a senior and very lovely. I was too shy back then to feel comfortable with the opposite sex. At the time, that was probably my loss. Danny and I would often ride together when he did not have farm work.

In the fall, my dad decided to take our horses to a property owned by a friend of his. The guy had some horses himself and said we could winter them over at his place. To this day, I really don't know exactly why. It may have been a money issue, for I was told to pick up the man's son on my way to school and then drop him off on my way home. I guess they were trading transportation for the boy with the cost of taking care of our horses. The arrangement was not very acceptable to me, for it was very inconvenient for me to ride Cricket. I was not about to say anything to my father about it.

About a month after this plan was in place, I returned home from school to find my father crying. He told me that Cricket had gotten into a fight with one of the other horses and had been badly hurt. I told him I would go over and see him, but dad said the vet had put him down. I was devastated and it would be years before I was able to forgive my dad for what he had, in a way, been responsible for. It was actually the first time I had ever seen my father cry and I should have been more mature about the accident. I was just so upset that I was not able to say good-bye to my "friend". I have owned several horses since, but I never got "close" to any of them like I had been with Cricket.

*

Lynda had two horses when we got married, a small, nasty pinto and a beautifully marked buckskin. She sold the pinto, since her girls were no longer interested in riding, and kept Pepper. I owned a big appaloosa mare at the time.

Pepper was acquiring the very bad habit of dislodging her rider, Lynda, who was in turn, getting tired of being bucked off. We traded Pepper, along with some cash to Ron and Terry Shurtz for two quarter horses, named Dee and Sadie. Not long after that horse-trading deal, my horse, Keebler, became ill and we had to put her down. We still had two good horses, so things were fine....for awhile.

We had gone on trail rides with Ron and Terry, but they liked to go on rides where they would camp overnight. We were just set up for day trips. We needed a bigger trailer if we were to stay longer. I had seen a flyer about an estate sale in Haysville, KS. Along with the house and "stuff" was a stock trailer.

I could not get away for the start of the sale, but I did go to the location to look at the trailer. It was old and not fancy at all, but it was in decent shape. Lynda agreed to go to the sale and bid on the trailer, if I did not make it there on time. I told her not to bid over $1,200.

Lynda was a bit nervous about the bidding, so she talked Terry into going with her. I showed up as soon as I could, but the crowd was past the trailer and auctioning off the furniture. I looked around for the gals and soon spotted Lynda. She was by the horse that had been pictured on the sale bill. As I got close to her, I saw a big smile on her face. She handed me a halter and said, "This is for your new horse. His name is Ace."

Yes, she had bought the horse. Did she buy the trailer? No, but she had reasons for both actions. I was too much in shock to get angry, so I just listened. At my age now, I have learned to listen, since it does no good to get angry.

I heard it *from the horse's mouth,* that there was this guy who hung around the horse and had been bad mouthing it. If anyone came up to look at the horse he would say things like, "Looks to be lame to me." She didn't think much of it until the horse came up for sale. Who was bidding on it? You are right, the guy who had been putting it down. Lynda told me at that point she was not going to let the man buy the horse. The high bid was, ironically, $1,200. "O K," I weakly said, "How much did the trailer go for." Lynda replied that it went for $900. I knew better, but I had to know why she hadn't bought the trailer, as well as the horse.

Her story on that one pretty much equaled the other one, but in reverse. After a time, Lynda and another lady were the only bidders. The bid had reached $900. Lynda and the woman were standing right beside one another and Lynda asked her how much higher was she willing to go. The woman told her she was going up to $1,500. Lynda told the lady that she would save her some money. Lynda stopped bidding. I had to grin, for I knew the woman had pulled one over on my naive, but wonderful wife.

The kicker to the story was that the horse would not load in my two-horse trailer. Ron brought his larger trailer over to load him up and bring him home.

Ron brought Ace home and pulled into the barn area. Red was running around, but I thought nothing of it. We backed Ace out of the trailer and down the ramp. He had no sooner been unloaded when Red ran up behind him and pecked his back leg. It was to be his last. Ace immediately kicked Red and sent him flying. The rooster was a "goner". We never replaced him.

*

Time is money.

BUSINESS

There is always room at the top
*

When the cat's away, the mice will play

We have all probably seen examples of the previous saying happen in the workplace and have possibly been guilty of it ourselves. Before you "play" or goof off in the absence of your boss, make sure that your office spaces are not being monitored and taped by video cameras. Video taping in private and public is "IN" and you often are not aware of it or you may have forgotten about them being present.
*

Don't mix business with pleasure
*

"Drive your business; do not let your business drive you."

Benjamin Franklin
*

A bad workman blames his tools
*

Be kind to those you meet on the way up

> ***for you may meet them on the way down***
> ***Business before pleasure***

But then there is…..

All work and no play makes Jack a dull boy.

Jack and Jill come up a lot in old sayings, but I don't have a clue why.

*

Even with so many consumer protection laws being passed, the next example is just as appropriate today as before.

Let the buyer beware

[Let the buyer charge far beyond their ability to repay.]

Businesses, of course, have always wanted people to buy their goods. With the vast array of charge cards available to us, they are selling more on credit, whether we can afford the bills or not. There was a time when people were actually turned down for a credit card or a new car loan. What happens if I have maxed out all of my credit cards and can only afford the minimum monthly payment required? Maybe not all, but most of the credit card companies would simply raise my limit, so that I could charge more. Does that make good business sense? It must work out somehow, since it seems to be the norm.

*

A friendship founded on business is better than a business founded on friendship

*

Success is getting up one more time than you fall down

*

"Each success only buys an admission ticket to a more difficult problem."

Henry Kissinger

*

"Creditors have better memories than debtors."

Benjamin Franklin

*

American Express – "Don't leave home without it."

Lynda and I have over twenty credit cards. We certainly don't need that many. Fortunately there are several with no balances and several that we pay off each month, if we use them. At this time we do not have an American Express Card. I have received numerous offers through the mail to apply for one, but I place them in the circular file beside my desk for future disposal. To my knowledge, none of my extended family nor any of my close friends have one either.

I have seen American Express commercials on the TV, but other than the slogan, I don't really remember anything about them. I do recall how Master Card does a splendid marketing job to show the advantage for carrying their card.
A major upcoming event is often depicted, such as the Super Bowl, and a local business is promoted. At the

end of the commercial, the great sounding announcer says something like….. After the game, drop by Joe's for a great meal, but bring your Master Card, because Joe's doesn't accept American Express.

*

It's not what you know, but who you know

This is still a problem in business, but not as bad as it once was. The "good buddy" approach for promoting people within a business has brought on many discrimination lawsuits from people who were "passed over" for advancement. I can see both views on the subject. If I were turned down for a position or not promoted and I was more qualified than others were, I may be a little upset too. On the other hand, I could be the biggest jerk in the company and not moved up the ladder, because those who have the power to promote just can't stand me.

If you aren't part of the solution then you must be part of the problem

*

MOST IRRITATING NOISE #2

I am uncomfortable, at any time, with the sound of anyone crunching their ice from their drink.

Lynda tells me that I am irritated by any noise that I do not initiate, but that is not being fair.

*

When Lynda and I got married (1994), we traded in my old camping trailer and bought a one year old pop up camper. We went camping at least a

couple of weekends a month and some friends told us
of a private RV camp north of Wichita. We called and
made arrangements to visit the facility.

The campground was owned by a firm called
Thousand Adventures. They were part of the Coast
to Coast program. If we bought a membership,
we could camp at any CC campground around the
country for a nominal fee. We decided to join. The
plan cost about $3,000, but there was no charge for
life to stay at any of the sites owned by Thousand
Adventures.

TA owned five campgrounds in Kansas and
we camped at three of them. We particularly liked
one southeast of us, near the Oklahoma border. It
was only about an hour's drive away from home. We
camped there several times to finish off the season.

The following summer we took off again for
Colorado, with the Coast to Coast book in hand. It
would be a good source to locate some new places
to stay. Our original plans were to visit Durango via
Ouray. Due to the distance involved, we wanted to
stop for a few nights to break up the trip.

We found an RV camp near Gunnison, called
Blue Mesa Ranch. We checked in at the gate, paid
$4.00, and set up camp at a very nice spot among the
only mature trees on the site. We found out later how
we lucked out on the location. The treed area was set
aside for campers without air conditioning. At the

lodge we saw a notice that offered two free southwest barbeque dinners in exchange for a sales talk from the management. We signed up.

The dinner was delicious. We met with the rep after the meal. He welcomed us and got right to the point. He said he had noticed we were members of TA and asked if the hard times the company was facing had affected us. He informed us about many of TA's campgrounds were being sold to stay afloat. The camp where we had originally signed up was one of those sold.

He made us an offer to trade the TA camp membership with one to their camp. Blue Mesa was certainly nicer and we agreed. He gave us a credit for every dollar we had invested with TA towards a BMR membership. We still had the Coast to Coast package and could still go to any camps in the book, which included any TA sites still open.

After we had been home awhile, we packed up the camper and drove down to the TA camp we liked. We arrived at the gate only to find it locked and the camp sign removed.

We had made a good choice. We are able to visit Blue Mesa only during my summer vacation, but it was worth it in the end.

*

The buck stops here

It is unusual for people to stand up, take the responsibility, and deal with a situation. All too often many people would rather.....

Pass the buck
*

At a good bargain, think twice

In 1998, we received an offer to stay three days and two nights at the Lodges of Maple Creek, in Branson, Missouri. Along with the free lodging, were two tickets to a Branson show and two free meals at an area restaurant. There was only one requirement.

We had to agree to attend a sales promotion at the resort during our stay. Lynda and I talked it over and decided to take them up on their offer. I had no qualms about the arrangement and it seemed like a good idea to get away for a few days. The trip would certainly be a change of scenery, since the Wichita area, unlike that of Branson, is void of hills and forests. After all, what could go wrong?

We had a delightful time and even took a side trip to Silver Dollar City, since neither of us had been there for quite some time. The free show was Shoji Tabuchi and it was quite well done. We paid to go to Dolly Parton's Dixie Stampede Dinner and Show. The show was very enjoyable and we, along with the crowd of hundreds, was served a country style meal where we sat in a surprisingly very short time.

The condo provided us was very top of the line, with a fire place, sleeping loft, and hot tub. It was situated, along with other units, among mature trees. All too often developers tear down trees for ease in construction. It looked like the builders had worked to build within the framework of the native landscape. Everything ran smoothly until the sales pitch.

I paid little attention to all that was going on in the presentation, because "**I**" had no intention to "invest", as they put it, in their resort. It was a much different story when it came to Lynda. She thought the idea was wonderful. Do you see where this is leading? The sales lady was very friendly and good with her pitch. Most successful sales people have the knack to sway people.

She could have sold sand to an Arab

At any rate, (you guessed it) after a couple of hours of intense talk, the papers were drawn up; we signed them, and forked over $6,500. It would have been one thing if we were buying an actual property, but we were buying a right to stay in one of their condos for two weeks each year. If things would have been that simple the money may have been worth it. We could trade our weeks at Branson with someone else at another time share location. We could vacation, in theory, at a four-star facility anywhere in the United States. The time share principle gives you little or no rights if the company behind it goes bankrupt.

As luck would have it (bad luck that is), they did. We knew nothing about it until we called the resort about ten months later to book "our condo" for a two-week stay. All the phone numbers given us for the resort were "not in service". I was quite stunned. When I found out about the company's status I became very angry.

The left hand often doesn't know what the right hand is doing

I contacted Missouri's Attorney General's Office and received not much more than sympathy. They forwarded me some forms to fill out, but they were not too optimistic that we would ever get any money back from the "investment". I discovered, over the Internet, that the lodge has reopened. We never heard anything more. I am still angry.

*

After a job interview, have you been told.....

Don't call us, we will call you

Well, hang in there and.....

Always put your best foot forward
*
The customer is always right

It's a misnomer to think that the customer is always right, but the premise that the customer is very important is sound business sense. There are too many businesses with poor customer relations. A large part of the problem has to be the fault of the employees who are hired by the company. Too many people work for the money, do not care for the job, and have an "I'd rather not be here" attitude.

*

My salary with the Girl Scouts would not be viewed as impressive by most and I do wish I made more, but the job is rewarding in ways other than financial. The young girls who come to camp learn to experience life in a different environment than they find at home or school. I am convinced that Girl Scouting helps them become better adults.

I'm eligible to retire now under the "Rule of 80" and I should look for work that would be less physically demanding. After over twenty-three years as a Camp Ranger I have mixed emotions about leaving. Maybe I should just enroll to get my masters and see what is out there.

*

Too many chiefs and not enough Indians

Many people in the Girl Scout organization think they are my supervisor and they all have their own agendas. At some point in time, I will have to stand up and tell them I need more Indians.

It's all in a day's work

*

Necessity is the mother of invention

*

I have seen many products invented that certainly were not necessary, in my opinion.

*

I recently saw the results of a poll to the following question: What invention is most needed, but also hated? The top three vote getters were:

Cell Phones
Televisions
Alarm Clocks

I'm surprised home computers were not on the list. I do love the computer over the typewriter, but there are so many features on them that I can't remember how to properly use most of them.

*

Jack of all trades, master of none

*

She could have sold ice to an Eskimo

*

He could sell water to a man who's drowning

On the other side of the coin there is.....

He couldn't sell water in the desert

*

The check's in the mail

I use that saying in an honest way, but I can tell those I say it to don't believe me. I have received the dreaded call from a creditor informing me that they didn't receive my payment. On one occasion, I had sent out three checks for bills on the same day. Not one of the payments were ever received.

I went to my post office and explained the situation. The clerk thought he remembered seeing a notice about a postal truck having a wreck on the turnpike around the same date in question. When I tried to get more information from the main Wichita post office, they were not helpful. A woman told me that I should have registered my mail if I wanted it tracked. They would not own up to the fact that they might have lost my mail.

I sent one of those checks to a new credit card company. In order to obtain a lower interest rate, I had recently transferred a rather large sum from another card to theirs. I lost a year's free interest, since I was late with my payment. I also lost the premium interest rate for my balance transfer. The three late charges cost me over a hundred dollars. The added expense for a higher interest was difficult to figure, but it was also substantial.

*

Let's get the show on the road

*

Cut your loses

*

Get the lead out

*

Lead, follow, or get the heck out of the road

*

Seen but not heard.

CHILDREN and KIDS

A son is a son 'till he gets a wife, but a daughter's a daughter all the days of her life.

*

All – The word used by one's kids to denote how many of their friends get to have or do something that they are not permitted to do or have.

The actual truth usually relates to one or maybe two of their friends. Examples of the way a youth will use the word would be: "Mom, all of my friends have a cell phone." or "Dad, all seniors are getting new cars from their parents for graduation."

*

Children should be seen, but not heard

When my dad was around my sisters and I usually did not want to be seen or heard. He should have married someone who would have been happy without children. If that were the case, I suppose I would not be here. OK, King's X. I take it all back, since I like being around.

I never had any kids of my own. At times, I think of what it would have been like to have a little boy or girl to raise. Then all that comes to mind is a crying baby and dirty diapers, so the thought doesn't last very long. I made a vow to myself years ago not to do two things in my lifetime; change a diaper and dress up like a woman. I have managed to keep both promises and I feel confident for continued success.

*

Spare the rod and spoil the child

When kids have done wrong, they should be verbally reprimanded and punished for their conduct . All too often, in my opinion, the consequences are not strong or strict enough to prevent other wrongs, or even recurrences of the same indiscretions. What is the incentive to obey a rule if the penalty for the violation of a rule is trite? This applies to adults as well as kids.

I am not, repeat, not in favor of any form of physical punishment that would inflict bodily injury upon a child or older kid. A good smack on the butt, not a whipping, may be all that is ever necessary to get a son or daughter's attention.

I don't know when physical punishment was done away with in the public school systems (in Kansas, at least), but I was once the recipient from the working end of an oak paddle, swung with vigor, onto the sitting end of my anatomy. I would almost consider that form of punishment to be excessive, except for one reason. It worked. The thought of ever being sent back to the shop teacher for another "lesson" stayed with me. I was in the seventh grade at the time, so it would have been about 1960.

I really do wish teachers were allowed to dole out some kind of "attention getters" to their unruly students. In fact, I substituted in the high school today and wished I had been allowed to whack a few knuckles with a ruler to control a few freshmen.

*

Children and fools tell the truth
*

"Cutted" – A word used by primary school students to notify the teacher that someone cut in line.

In the primary school grades, the class is often required to leave the classroom for restroom breaks, recess, lunch, PE, library, computer, or music. Each one of those trips requires the kids to line up. If the teacher does not have an exact line up order, there is always a problem with the process. At least one student will get upset with another kid for cutting in line. This really is a big deal with many kids.

I get frustrated with those kids, who feel that a crime has been committed. I generally send all those involved to the back of the line for arguing, which really gets them fuming. I inform the little complainers that there will be many things in their future to worry about, so don't blow things out of proportion at this stage in their lives.

Don't sweat the small stuff
*

If I've told you once, I've told you a hundred times

My mother would direct the previous saying to me upon numerous occasions during my youth. It was usually in regards to not taking out the trash when needed or not cleaning up my room. I actually do not remember ever cleaning up my room. I am sorry, Mom. Lynda has scolded me, on occasion, for being messy or not picking up after myself. It must be a guy thing. I'm sorry, Lynda.

*

Batteries – The power supply required, but "not included" for many kid's toys, which costs more than the toy did in the first place.

*

MOST IRRITATING SOUND #3

The noise produced by a crying baby or child drives me up a wall. Women seem to be, at times, unaffected by a wailing baby or crying kid. Is it possible that a female can become immune to the sound?

I am confronted by the vial sound anywhere in public, of course, but one of the worst places is in a restaurant, right after the order has been placed. I have made the commitment to be there for a period of time, trapped, so to speak.

I am not as affected now as I used to be. I recall abandoning my partially filled shopping cart in a store, because of the noise. I had to seek the safety of the parking lot. I have found a benefit for those markets open 24/7. The chance of running into a shopping mother, wielding a crying infant, in the late evening is pretty slim.

*

The terrible two's – The excuse given by parents to somehow explain the poor temperament of a child.

The female parent will always make excuses for why their child is acting up. If it isn't because they are tired, hungry, bored, or some other ailment, it is just the stage they are going through. Well, they seem to be going through one stage or another for their entire lives.

Boys will be boys and **Girls will be girls**

*

Don't throw the baby out with the bath water

*

Watch your step.

The COLORADO ROCKIES

I had done a fair amount of hiking in the high country of Colorado before Lynda and I married. The scenery of the forests and being out in nature was spectacular. On one trip, for some reason, I stopped at a scenic overlook on the way to Winter Park, CO, and began to hike. It was in August of 1988 and I was near Berthoud Pass. I ventured past the forest and made it to the top of Stanley Mountain, at 12,521 feet (I didn't know what it was or how high it was at the time). The hike and climb had been exhausting. On the summit, I was surprised to find a foot-long plastic canister with a register inside. Those who had been there before me had signed it.

I put my business card, a five-dollar bill, and a note inside an empty black film container. I placed it in the canister. I wrote "Congratulations, you made it to the top" on the note. I had been home from the vacation for a few weeks and one day, to my surprise,

I received a letter from a woman named Mary Parker, who had found the "reward".

Mary was from the Denver area. She had hiked Stanley a few days after me and found the film container. She thought it was only litter and was going to throw it away after she returned home. She just happened to open it before throwing it away and was pleasantly surprised to fine the cash and note. We wrote back and forth occasionally for quite some time. She was surprised to learn that I had never climbed any 14'ers. I didn't even know what one was back then. I may never have climbed a 14'er if Mary hadn't jump started my interest. I am glad I decided to take the challenge.

*

I would like to take the time to make the distinction between "climbing" and "hiking". There is a difference. Most of the distance covered from the trailhead to the summit is accomplished by hiking. Climbing encompasses that final 1,000 to 1,500 feet of elevation gain and is usually a real test of endurance. Technical climbing is a **different ballgame** and requires the use of harnesses and ropes, but I am not trained in that area. Biking and stair climbing are two exercises that are good for getting in shape for mountain hiking/climbing. The final accent is like a stairway a mile long.

I won't present a story of every 14'er that I have climbed, but I will recount portions of some of the trips. I took on the personal challenge to climb 14'ers to prove something to myself. It wasn't, as some have said.....

Because they are there

Colorado is, if you haven't guessed it by now, my favorite state and climbing the magnificent and equally imposing fourteeners has to be one of my most rewarding experiences in life. I have hiked, climbed, and/or crawled to the summits of twenty-four of them.

In a technical sense, fifty-four mountains in the state are considered 14'ers, which is short for those whose summits are 14,000 feet (or higher) in elevation above sea level. Most of the higher peaks in the state will have an elevation gain of three to five thousand feet from the trailhead to the summit. There are two 14'ers that one can drive to the top. I have hiked, driven, and ridden the cog train to the summit of Pike's Peak. Hiking it was more fun.

The first 14'er I conquered (Aug. 16, 1989) was Mt. Princeton and I was prepared to call it quits after the twelve hour, seven mile journey with a 5,400 foot elevation gain. After that, I did my homework and picked some easier ones. A few were close enough to each other that one could hike two or three on the same excursion. Now don't get me wrong, they were not all *a piece of cake*, but some were certainly not as difficult as others. For a Kansas "flatlander" they were all memorable.

I feel that I have to mention something about the second 14'er on my list. I was really beat after Princeton. The next day I drove from my campsite at Collegiate Peaks Campground, into the nearby town of Buena Vista. I just happened to see a copy of the Aug. 17th edition of the "Chaffee County Times". In it was an article about a man from Massachusetts who had fallen to his death a week earlier, while climbing Mt. Yale.

I was a little bit stunned, for I had chosen Yale as my next attempt. The trailhead for Yale began just across the road from my campground. It must have been fate or something for me to have selected Princeton first over Yale. The man had lost his balance while crossing a snow field and slid about 300 feet down across ice and snow then another 300 feet over rocks. He had "died of massive head and internal injuries." Two witnesses had tried to assist him, but to no avail. He was taken out by helicopter.

I still climbed Yale the next day and I believe I came to where the man had fallen. There was a 100 foot wide snowfield in a depression near the summit. It was in a shaded area and had not melted. To cross it would save time reaching the top. The outer edges were soft, but a few feet in, towards the middle, it was ice. I decided to make the detour up and around the obstacle. I have made it a point never to cross snowfields without a pick axe and metal boot cleats.

Mt. Antero is 14,269 feet and 10th on the highest in Colorado list. Antero is known as the "gem mountain", due to the vast amount of gems that have been discovered on it since the late 1800's. The day I climbed it I ran into a group of modern day prospectors. They looked like they could have been from 1890. The only difference actually was their up to date tent and camping supplies. They searched for gems virtually the same way it was done by those prospectors one hundred years before…...by hand.

I struck up a conversation with the trio of "diggers" and they said if I had nothing better to do I could help sift through soil for gems. It sounded like a good way to take a break from my descent, so I agreed. Evidently one must apply for a permit to look for the gems. You can't just go out and legally dig up a mountain side. I found a few crystals while I was there and they gave me a few imperfect gems as souvenirs.

*

In August of 1993, before Lynda and I were wed, we took a trip to, of course, Colorado. We really have visited other places. She wanted to experience the climb of a 14'er. We were taking a southern route through the state along highway 160 and had planned to stay overnight at the Great Sand Dunes National Forest Campground.

The campground was virtually treeless, at that time, so it wasn't very picturesque. The exhibit about the sand dunes at the U.S. Park Service office was interesting, especially if you were into geology and, of course, sand. We spent the afternoon walking around in the huge mountain of sand, with the nearby Sangre de Cristo mountain range in view. Our plans were to challenge Blanca Peak and, if time permitted, to cross over to another 14'er, Mt. Ellingwood.

Blanca Peak, at 14,345 feet, is Colorado's 4th highest mountain. We started out on the right foot, for we set out early. We pulled off the highway onto a dirt road to the trailhead. We bounced along to an area where some other vehicles were parked. The road did go on farther, but it looked very rough and Lynda's van was certainly not the vehicle of choice to follow it. We had purchased a video camera and planned to tape the trek. The novelty of it was fun, but we messed around and wasted too much time recording instead of hiking. We would not realize that until later.

We reached the beautiful area of Lake Como. We would have enjoyed it much more had it not been for millions of mosquitoes who were there to great us. O.K., I exaggerate, but there were a lot of them. Neither one of us had brought along repellent, so we admired the scenery for only a brief time.

We didn't make it to the summit until 5:00 p.m. We had begun the trip at 8:00 a.m. The goofing around earlier was to haunt us now. We were greeted at the top by a nasty storm front. There was no time to rest for I knew we should get down ASAP. We stayed only long enough to sign the register. I also presented Lynda with a "Blanca Peak" pin to commemorate her first 14'er conquest. It had begun to rain with sleet mixed in for added measure.

The trip down was slow and hazardous. The rocks and boulders acquire a moss or other vegetative growth, which is not particularly noticeable until you walk on them when they are wet. It was like trying to walk down a slope of ice.

In the higher elevations rain, sleet, or snow is one thing, but lightening is quite another. It is a major concern for any mountain hiker going above timber line, which is generally at about 12,500 feet. Timber line is the area where the elevation is so high trees do not grow. Storm fronts frequently hit the Rockies in the early afternoon. Hikers, summits, and storms is not a good combination.

It was dark by the time we made it back to Como Lake. We (I) had also neglected to bring any sort of flashlight along. We came across a nice group of folks at the lake, who had backpacked up to stay overnight. They were so helpful. We had run out of water and food. They gave us both and thankfully let us use a flashlight. I hate to think how hard it would have been to continue the trip down without one.

They had parked near our van and gave us a description of their vehicle. I put a five dollar bill and the flashlight beside one of the tires as a tip for their kindness. In looking back on the incident, I should have left a twenty. We reached the van at 10:30 p.m., which was a "day hike" of fourteen and a half hours.

I will have to take responsibility for all the problems we encountered. I knew that one should plan to reach any summit much earlier and I could have been better prepared for the possibility of being in the dark. As far as the water goes, I didn't realize Lynda would drink so much. From experience in the past, I found I could do fine with only a quart of water, which is the heaviest item a hiker will carry. We took only two quarts with us. I also found that Lynda needed much more energy food than I was accustomed to having. I only took two candy bars. She had trail mix, but it didn't go far.

In our subsequent long hikes together I reluctantly carry much more than I would like to. The water and food issue was compound in our hikes later, since we have had Cricket and usually one of my dogs along. We had to take water and food for them as well. I came up with a plan to reduce the load during part of the hike. I carry a "drop off" pack with water and food to be left when the hike becomes a climb and picked up later on the way back.

Lynda and I were married in Breckenridge, CO, in '94. One of the events planned while staying there was to climb Quandary Peak, which was not too far south. Preparations had been made for the climb the day after the wedding. I remembered to include the "drop off" pack, with extra water, food, **and** a flashlight.

The trip was routine, with the burning lungs, sore feet, aching legs, and other assorted body pains. We were at the top when we noticed a sign which read "North Star – 13,614 ft." Sure as #*?!# we were on the wrong mountain. As we looked to the north we could see another mountain higher than we were. O.K., I'll take the blame for that goof up too.

Talk is cheap.

COMMUNICATION

Talk is cheap

*

Put your money where your mouth is

*

Talk – What kids do in school and on into their adult lives when they should be listening

*

Lynda and I have, at this writing, been taking classes to learn how to sign. She has, in turn, allotted a portion of her class time schedule to teach the kids the basics of signing. She tells me they are excited to learn something that is new to most of them. Lynda works extra hard to make learning fun for her kids.

*

Actions speak louder than words

[Those who talk a lot often do little]

*

It's not what you say, but how you say it

*

Fools ask questions that wise men cannot answer

*

The pen is mightier than the sword
This one could have been said by a politician

Ask no questions and I'll tell you no lies

[Ask no questions and you will get no answers]
*
If the shoe fits wear it

[If the shoe fits, buy the same size next time.]
*
Do as I say, not as I do

[Do as I say, not as I do, or you will be as screwed up as I am.]
*
Advice when most needed is less heeded
*

The advances in telecommunications are amazing. I am really impressed with the new technology. There appears to be no end to what the technical field can do, but I feel they have often gone far enough.

Lynda talked me into signing up for a cell phone when she obtained one, as if people didn't have enough ways to communicate with me already. I have a home phone, work phone, and an extension at the council and they all have answering machine capability. I have work email, home email, and a pager. Now I have a cell phone. It has become a chore just to check for my messages. Some overly efficient, cover all of the bases type, individuals will leave the same message on my entire menagerie of message taking devices.

I would prefer only using my cell phone for emergencies if we were driving somewhere. I didn't really need nor did I want my phone to take, transmit, and receive pictures or tell me when it was time to go to the bathroom. I certainly didn't want a 190 page booklet telling me how to use the damn thing.

It's Greek to me
*

Whatever happened to Jeff Foxworthy who coined....

Here's your sign
*

Read my lips
*

Get your mind out of the gutter
*

Did I stutter?
*

Whatever!

My youngest daughter, Tana, frequently used the word in her conversations with me, usually in conjunction with a disagreement of some sort. When I would hear her utter the word, I knew the verbal exchange between us was over.

Speak softly and carry a big stick
*

I hope no one takes what I have to say personally, but that will remain to be seen. The topic has to do with music. The radio is, most certainly, a very much needed form of communication. Lynda listens to the same station every morning while she gets ready for work. I never was one to spend much time listening to music on the radio or on any other type of audio noise maker. I find noise to be distractive to my way of concentration.

*

I always detested the "twangy" voices of the past country and western singers. They have finally disappeared and I do enjoy many of the new country sounds. Faith Hill and Shania Twain and other female vocalists of country are really quite good.

I'm not saying the guys are not good, but I am really not into watching guys sing country and western.

*

When "rap" first hit the air the sound was unique, which it was, but as time wore on the uniqueness wore off. I wish it would disappear as well. I dislike the lyrics more than I do the music. The words are often nothing but a collection of profane and distasteful utterances.

*

When all men speak, no man hears

*

Tell it like it is

I have been in the dog house at home, on the carpet at work, and just plain disliked by many, who don't want to hear it like it is.

Profanity –Words, written or spoken, that are not considered proper for everyday usage.

In many movies the script calls for the use of the "F" word. Often times, in my opinion, it is used far too frequently. Swear or cuss words may have a limited role in our language, but communication can certainly do without many of them.

My father used to swear a lot in his talk, but I only heard him say the "F" word once in front of me, and he actually apologized for saying it. I didn't like him swearing constantly, which was one reason why we kids were inclined not to bring friends over. I am impressed with those who don't cuss.

*

Why? – The favorite word of three-year-olds

I often have to be careful what I say when I substitute in school, since I have not successfully been able to rid my speech of all expletives. One can always replace a swear word with a variety of words.

*

Practice what you preach

*

80

While on the subject of the English language, I thought I'd interject a thought I have had for a long time. Why are there so damn (just kidding) many words in the dictionary? Does there really need to be over a thousand pages in a dictionary? I don't really think so. I had to look up "expletives" and happened to catch sight of "expostulation". In part of the wordy definition was the word "remonstrate". Now seriously, do we really need all of those words? I still don't think so. If a guy came up to my wife and wanted to expostulate with her on a matter, I hope she would smack him one.

*

Our forefathers did foul one thing up when we broke from England. We should have come up with an "American" language with our own separate dictionary. We could have started spelling words like they sounded, which is one of my biggest complaints concerning the English language.

*

Silence is golden

I will have to settle for silver, because I can't seem to keep my big trap shut or at least get it closed before I say too much.

*

I have noticed that some pre-school teachers talk to adults as if they were their pre-school kids.

*

Don't shoot the messenger

*

Put up or shut up

81

*

You've sure said a mouthful

*

The handwriting is on the wall

*

"He can compress the most words into the smallest idea of any man I know."

Abraham Lincoln

One of my good friends is Neil Boyce. He is also employed by the Girl Scout and is the Ranger of our resident camp in the flint hills of Kansas. Neil has to be at the top of the nice guys in the world list, if there were such a list. I really get cracked up when I hear or see those words that good 'ole Abe said. Neil, bless his soul, must have been reborn, because the quote *fits him to a "T"*. If I ever need to call him for any reason I always make sure I have plenty of time to talk or I should say listen.

In one ear and out the other

*

I told you so

*

If you have nothing nice to say, say nothing

*

MOST IRRITATING NOISE #4

It is sad to hear young people use foul, dirty, language and think they are "cool", because it's not.

Too many irons in the fire.

DECISIONS or CHOICES

We have all been in *Catch 2* situations where any decision we made turned out to be the wrong one. It's closely related to.....

Damned if you do, damned it you don't
*
Flip a coin
*
Heads I win, tails you lose

When I was a young "nerd" I had that trick pulled on me along with the two headed and two tailed coins. I finally wised up after loosing my lunch money on numerous occasions.
*
Of two evils, pick the least
*
There's more than one way to skin a cat
*
Don't burn the candle at both ends

Too many of us do it because either we don't know how to delegate, have too much to do, or we are workaholics. I work from daylight into the dark during the spring, summer, and fall. I do try to rest during the winter to even out the hours some, but that plan doesn't work as well as I would like.

*

Like it or lump it

*

When in doubt, do nothing

There must be a lot of people in this world who are often in doubt, or it may be just an excuse to be lazy.

*

You can run, but you can't hide

I believe that one is the theme of "America's Most Wanted"

*

Where there's a will, there's a way

I went by the nickname of "Will" for a number of years during my duty in Hawaii and later in Vietnam. When I first checked into the squadron at Barber's Point, on Oahu, the E-4 checking me in said, "Not another one."

There were so many guys with the name of "Ray" or Raymond", that other alternatives were already taken. Along with those two given names, there was a "Big Ray", "Little Ray", and even an "X-Ray". He informed me that I needed to go by "Will" (short for William, my middle name). He said that I should be called "Big Ray", since I was actually bigger than him, but I took it in stride and rather liked the "new" *handle.*

*

Ray Racobs

Don't drink and drive

[Don't drive with those who drink]

*

Never put off till tomorrow what you can do today

There are a few people who must have gotten this one mixed up and think it is…..

Put off today what you can do tomorrow
*
Six of one, half a dozen of another
*
Sink or swim
*
It's your funeral
*
You have to take the bad with the good
*
I've got places to go, people to see, and things to do
*
The mind is willing, but the flesh is weak
*
When you come to a fork in the road, take it
*
If it's not broken, don't fix it
*
Don't open that can of worms
*

Take it or leave it

86

*

There are several sayings that deal with burning things up, but burning bridges is a no…no…

Don't burn your bridges before you get there

Don't burn your bridges behind you

[Don't burn your bridges while you are on them]

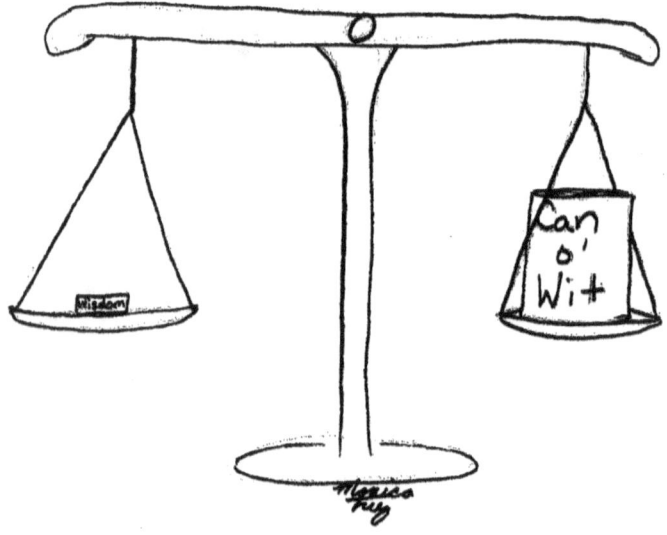

An ounce of wisdom is worth a pound of wit.

EDUCATION

A little knowledge is a dangerous thing

Knowledge is power
*
Experience is the best teacher

[Experience is the best teacher, but it doesn't help your GPA.]

I went to Kansas State University, right out of high school, way back when. I was raised in a household with a rather strict father in charge of our family's every move. When I went to college, it was the first time in my life that I was not controlled by someone. I experienced "life". I learned how to drink beer, smoke cigarettes, drink beer, stay up all night, and drink beer. After the first full year there, my grade point average was .02, which is not a typo. It was a .02 not a 2.0. It took me years to really mature, but I finally did. I would obtain my degree 32 years later, but graduate with honors. So.....

It's better late than never
Great minds think alike

I don't know about the "great", but Lynda and I think
so much alike it is, at times, almost scary.

*

Those who can do, those who can't, teach

I don't know who the ignorant jerk was who
first uttered those words. Maybe I'm missing some
context. This would be my first choice of old sayings
that could be eliminated from use. It is not just
because my wife teaches either. Teachers do not get
near enough credit for what they do and what they
have to put up with. I could go on in some length
about this, but won't. I am sure that the intelligent
people in the country admire and respect teachers.

[If you are too old to do something any longer, then
teach it to someone who can]

A friend of mine thought the saying meant
something like I proposed. If that was the case, they
should have been a little more specific.

*

Experience without learning is better than learning

without experience
*

"I have never let schooling interfere with my education."

Mark Twain
*

Everyone is wise after the fact
*

Hindsight is 20/20
*

There are quite a few proverbs that are inclined to belittle ones intelligence.

He doesn't have both oars in the water

He's not playing with a full deck

There's a sucker born every minute
*

When I substitute any class for the first time, I can generally tell, within a few minutes, how well the teacher controls his or her students. There are two things that I pay particular attention to.

The first one deals with the condition or appearance of the classroom. If the room is rather cluttered and disorganized I see trouble ahead. If the class is neat and orderly chances are I will have a good day. In my mind, there appears to be a direct correlation between the look of the classroom and the attitude of the students.

The second observation I make occurs during the first few moments after the bell rings. One would expect the class to quiet down shortly after the tardy bell sounds. This isn't always the case.

On one occasion, in high school, the class was very disruptive before the bell rang. I decided to see how long it would take them to settle down. The bell rang and I just sat behind the desk and looked out among the students. I got tired of the noise after nine minutes and had to restore order to the room. I still wonder if they would ever have calmed down.

*

An ounce of wisdom is worth a pound of wit

*

You are never too old to learn

[You are not the "old dog".]

*

It was not an early goal of mine to obtain a degree over and above my associate's degree. It was very interesting to attend college as an adult. I first worked on retaking all of the classes where I had failed or done poorly. Generally I was older than most of the instructors. I did go ahead and obtain my bachelor's degree for several reasons. First was for Mom. She can brag that all of her kids were college graduates. She was very proud of me and I was elated to make her happy.

Lynda had obtained her teaching degree and I couldn't let her be more educated. Seriously, I knew I could not be a Camp Ranger forever and felt I must prepare for a second career. I would rather have had a degree that would allow me to teach, but I could not do the semester of internship with my employment. The state began to allow schools to hire those who weren't certified, if they enrolled in night school and obtained certain education classes. When I was ready to apply for a teaching position the state changed the wavier rule. Well…..

He who hesitates is lost

In a way, I feel the time and money expended will not be worth the achievement. An individual in their late fifties is not nearly as hirable. I would be an excellent teacher, but may never get the chance.

I tell many students in high school to buckle down, don't party like I did, and get through college before they get into situations that will delay their education.

*

In a recent conversation with one of the paras at the high school the subject of college arose. She was taking classes to further her qualifications in the field of Special Education. She told me about her psychology professor, whose vocabulary was so far advanced that she and others couldn't understand what was being said.

This, in my opinion, would be an individual who falls into the category of being "an educated idiot". If those types of people think they are being admired for their mastery over the dictionary, they are wrong, because they don't fit in the real world.

I have known some people like that, but I certainly don't go out of my way to associate with them. I often feel like they are trying to impress me with their knowledge of the English language. Well, I'm not impressed, but I do feel sorry for them.

*

There are some who know a little, but think they know a lot

*

In many of the books that are required reading in primary school, the vocabulary is too advanced for their age level. It is not enjoyable for me to read a book for pleasure and have to augment it with the dictionary sitting on my lap.

*

I asked one of my friends to read a portion of the book and give me his honest opinion as feedback. He said he liked what he read (I did give him some chapters that I felt were more interesting than others), but he thought authors weren't supposed to write using contractions.

I do recall something to the fact way back in English Composition at KSU. I then remembered my least favorite professor in all of my education. I will also never forget some of the exact words he said in the first class. He had been going over the syllabus and ended by saying, "If you flunk the final, you flunk the class." I asked him, "Can I take the final now?" He said, "What?" Then I proceeded to explain. "If I took the final now and flunked, then I wouldn't have wasted the whole semester of coming to class."

It didn't go over too well with him. I was only being realistic. When I would get my papers back from him there were red marks all over them. I could have sworn that he had taped my essays to the front of his car and run into deer on the highway. I had a C+ going into the final, which I flunked. A big surprise it wasn't. He was true to his word….. for I did flunk the class. I should have protested to the school administration, but there was no such thing as student rights back in '64.

Oh, I almost forgot. I (and we) speak using contractions. If it were for a grade, I probably **would not** use them, but **it's** not. I remind you again….It's my book. If e. e. cummings can write without capital letters and get away with it, then.....

To each his own

*

Too many cooks.

FOOD

Don't bite the hand that feeds you
*
Don't bite off more than you can chew

Dessert – A food, usually sweet in taste, which is eaten after the meal, unless you are an adult. Then it can be eaten any darn time you want.

You can't have your cake and eat it too
*
Cereal - A food item normally consumed in the morning for the breakfast meal.

As a young kid (and actually ate breakfast), it seemed there was a very good assortment of cereals available at the local grocery store. In my family, we usually had corn flakes, grits or oatmeal, but I didn't mind. These varieties are, of course, still sold. What blows my mind are the choices available today.

I was headed to Dillon's, a large food store in our area, and Lynda asked me to pick her up a box of

Kellogg's Oat and Nuts. When I came to the cereal section, I was shocked to see how many selections there were along one entire, long, aisle. I suppose I have never paid any attention to how many cereal brands and types are sold, since I don't eat cereal anymore.

I must have been very bored that particular day, because I started to count the number of choices available. There were 169, and that didn't include the hot cereals on the other side of the aisle or different sized boxes of the same brand variety.

*

The way to a man's heart is through his stomach

*

Too many cooks spoil the soup (or stew)

*

Asparagus – A poor excuse for a food source, even if it is a vegetable

*

A half a loaf of bread is better than no bread at all

*

One rotten apple will spoil all in the barrel

*

Tossed salad – Rabbit food

*

Deep pan, hand tossed, or original

*

Eat, drink, and be merry

*

"No clock is more regular than the belly"
Benjamin Franklin

Ray Racobs

MOST IRRITATING NOISE # 5

I hate the sound of people eating noisy food, such as chips, when I am not eating.

I don't know why this social malady of mine came about, but I know I wasn't annoyed by food noise when I was younger. I am normally not at all bothered by the sound when I am eating with others. If I were in charge of the snack or salad tray, I would not include celery, carrots, or crackers. I would prefer Twinkys, marshmallows, or sugar donuts. At meal time I don't mind other noises, such as the TV, radio, or conversation.

*

I enjoy going to almost any type of eating establishment that offers all you can eat buffets. I know I will not leave hungry, but at times, when I have eaten too much, I wish I had remembered.......

The eyes are bigger than the stomach
*
Your plate is full
*
Greatest thing since sliced bread
*
Who the cook is doesn't matter when one is hungry

*

Three faithful friends.

FRIENDS

"A friend to all is a friend to none."
Aristotle
*

The true measure of a man is how he treats someone who can do him absolutely no good

It was to my surprise that I heard this saying a few days after I had struck up a short conversation with a gentleman at the local Dollar General Store. We spoke for some time about nothing, really. I don't know why I started talking to him in the first place. I usually am friendly, and the guy just looked like a nice person. It made me feel good about myself for going out of my way to be nice.
*

Women: *Can't live with 'em, can't live without 'em*

I am sure that saying has generally been used in fun, but just in case it wasn't, I only agree with the second half. I enjoy the company of Lynda and when she isn't home for some reason or another, I miss her.

One good friend is a lot, two are many, and three almost impossible
*

A friend in need is a friend indeed
*

"I never met a man I didn't like."
Will Rogers

Having no long term friends was a problem associated with moving around when I was young. The same was true while in the Navy. A tour of duty was often short and people were always coming and going. In Vietnam it was the same story, but with an added problem. One didn't seem to go out of their way to establish any meaningful friendships. This was especially true in combat areas. I cannot recall a single person's name while I was stationed there.

I had no true friends until I became the Ranger at Camp Seikooc. I was there 20 years and made many friends, but my best friend was (and is still today) Gary Elliott. He was my shift Captain in the fire department and conveniently lived across the road. We could always rely on each other if we needed any help on anything.

Moving away from where I had lived for so long was one thing. Leaving my best friend, who I saw every day, was another. We still manage to get together on occasion, but not as frequently as we both would like.

*

"There are three faithful friends – an old wife, an old dog, and old money."

Benjamin Franklin

*

An enemy of my enemy is my friend

This is the main reason that we never directly went to war with Russia.

*

Forgive and forget

*

One good turn deserves another

*

You scratch my back and I'll scratch yours

*

Better to be alone than in bad company

Even when I drank and partied more often than one should, I hung out with respectable people. Some of them had a drinking problem like me, but they were decent folk. We didn't go around and get into trouble. We weren't destructive nor mean. We were just a bunch of fun loving souls.

*

Since we frequent Blue Mesa Ranch each summer, we have made many long term friends that we only see for a short time. That could be a good thing. All too often, the better one knows another, the less they end up liking each other.

[If you are remembered by many, you have been either very good or very bad]

*

As much as I have mentioned Blue Mesa in the book, maybe it is a place for you to put on your travel plans. If you become a member it would be nice if you told them I referred you. At one time members were given money for referrals. If I reap any monetary gain I'll split it with you.

Blue Mesa is owned by Western Horizon Resorts. They have at least eighteen RV and cabin sites in nine states, mostly in the west, southwest, and south. BMR is the only property owned by them that we have visited.

*

All for one and one for all

The *Three Musketeers,* by Dumas, made that one famous and Walt Disney made a movie in the early '90's with the same title.

*

The more one gets, the more one wants.

GIFTS

Cash – A substitute for a "real" gift, for any occasion, that requires absolutely no effort nor thought, but is warmly received by all

*

Gift Certificate – A popular gift, for any occasion, that requires a little effort and a little thought and is usually accepted graciously

*

Candle – A popular gift, for any occasion, that requires a little effort, but absolutely no thought and often seems to be appreciated by those who get one

I would not suggest giving a candle to a real guy.

*

Fear those bearing gifts

That one has been around ever since the Trojan horse story.

*

The best things come in small packages

OK, guys, what comes in small packages?

Diamonds are a girl's best friend
High Maintenance – The term is often used when
referring to the cost of keeping a female happy

Over the years, I have come up with a few
cues that will, with good accuracy, determine if a
woman is high maintenance. If a woman adorns
herself with diamond jewelry just to go to the mall,
she should be required to wear a red flag in plain
view. These are quite often the ones who take up
two parking spots with their BMW, Porsche, or some
other expensive vehicle. I guess.....

If you've got it, flaunt it

Women who wear up to five gold rings (at the
same time) and assorted gold jewelry would be in the
next bracket for guys to watch out for. Now don't get
me wrong. I see nothing wrong with women dressing
up to make themselves look attractive, but there are
things to pay attention to when a guy is looking for a
mate.

I feel most men out there would be much
more comfortable with a woman, who wears silver
jewelry, does not drink, drives a mid-sized car, prefers
a burger to a steak, and likes to wear jeans. Did I
describe my wife? Well, pretty much so. I never said
that I wasn't opinionated. She's not perfect, but I'm
not either.

*

Don't look a gift horse in the mouth

Some of you may not get that one. I'll explain it the way I see it. A rancher or experienced horse person can look into a horse's mouth and tell about how old a horse is. In other words, the saying implies that it is not proper to "knock" or put down something that was a gift. With that in mind.....

It is not good to refuse a gift

Now I have never refused a gift, but I have probably accepted some with little or no enthusiasm. I have received some "dumb" gifts in my life and I will not pretend to like them. Right away I recall a Christmas gift from my Aunt Betty in 2002. I opened my gift with smiles and anticipation. The smile soon became a frown. I found that the contents yielded a depiction of the three monkeys......

See no evil, hear no evil, speak no evil

I looked at her in confusion. The box showed a different scene on each of its sides. Aunt Betty thought the gift was a scene of three bears, but she had only noticed the side with the bears. The side with the three monkeys was checked, denoting that the contents were the monkeys. It was an honest mistake. The whole affair ended up being a good laugh for all.

*

I put aside money each payday in a Christmas club account at the bank. My yearly goal is $1,000 and I have achieved it every year since opening the account. I try to impress upon Lynda that we should not go over the amount saved and not charge any gifts, but to no avail. She uses her own money to buy gifts as well as charging gift purchases. The whole process of planning and setting a budget seems to be a loosing battle. By the time I get the credit balances back under control the holiday season is upon us once more.

*

It is better to give than to receive

Well, if the story about my views on gifts got me into warm water, this one should fire the water up to being suitable enough for the hot tub. I have three choices I suppose. I could stay in the skillet and fry, jump into the fire, or just take the idea out of the book. The third choice is the easiest, but.....

God hates a coward

First off, I agree that it is better to give only in the sense of giving to a charity or someone truly in need. In that scenario, I would not expect anything in return. I do not agree with the premise as it stands. I do not feel that the saying has merit, even if it is not directly related to gifts. Is it better to give kindness or love to another and get nothing in return? Maybe for awhile, but not for long.

What I have to say next does not refer to any of the relatives on Lynda's side of the family. They are always more than willing to give no matter what their financial situation is. A few of my relation are unwilling to give everyone in the family a Christmas gift. I am more than likely going to step on a few toes with all I have to say, but so be it.

In my distorted and twisted mind, I feel there is no reason good enough, which would excuse any of my family not to give a Christmas gift to everyone in the immediate family. The family consists of only fourteen members. Evidently many of them think the old saying goes.....

It is better to receive than give.

I have shared my opinions with my mother who always gives plenty of gifts, even when she is on a fixed income. I told her that I did not care if one went out in the yard, picked up a pinecone, spread peanut butter on it, and gave it to me as a bird feeder. At least it would be a gift of some kind. I do not expect much, but I do expect something.

Maybe this will set some of them straight when they read my book. Of course I will have to give them one, since they are certainly too hard up to purchase a copy of it. Maybe I will just give them one as next years Christmas gift. What an idea.

*

What comes around goes around

I must tell a story about one "non-giver". The individual was my younger sister's husband, Jerome. I never did call him brother-in-law, for I feel one has the option to accept or refute any in-law as relation. It's my own rule, but.....

It works for me.

While Jerome and Pam were married we never received any gifts from them, but they had always been happy to receive gifts. I had thought he was a Jehovah Witness member, but later learned that he wasn't. That didn't set well with me, so one year I nicely wrapped up a box of nothing and sent it home with Pam for Jerome. That's right, the box contained nothing. I would have given almost anything to have seen the look on his face when he opened it. Lynda, of course, thought I had been very rude. I'm glad she knew nothing of my plan, for she would surely have intercepted the package.

That was quite a few years ago, but I still get a big laugh out of it when my memory pulls the story out of the files. There is, of course, a large financial demand on everyone during the holidays. Families grow and the monetary commitment increases.

The more one gets, the more one wants
*

Death and taxes.

GOVERNMENT

All men are created equal

I always thought it ironic that the founders of our great country and of the Constitution felt so strongly about those words, even though many of the signers didn't believe it for a minute and never would. If all men were truely "created" equal, they didn't remain equal for long.

*

Power tends to corrupt and absolute power corrupts absolutely

In my heart, mind, and soul I truly feel that the United States is the greatest country in the world. What bothers me is the fact that we could be so much better. Our governmental system, when formed, with built in checks and balances was sound in theory, but it has not worked out as well today as it should.

*

Politics makes strange bedfellows

*

The number of unbelievable stories of waste, corruption, and incompetence are endless. We see or hear about them virtually every night on the evening news, but things don't get better. Being a citizen is frustrating to me, but it certainly could be worse.

The election process is almost a joke. The vast majority of our citizens have the right to vote, but don't. I don't fall for the ideological pretext that every vote counts. Only one vote counts and that is the one that gives one person a majority over another.

The politician will say one thing to one part of the population and something different to others. Most of those in political positions are not willing to vote for what is right if it alienates those special interest groups who really elected them. We should be voting on the issues that directly pertain to our lives instead of someone with their own agenda. We should decide where our tax dollars go. Too many of those elected don't care about the "silent majority" after they are elected to office.

*

United we stand, divided we fall

*

Even enemies have something in common

*

"The way to slow down old age is to move it through Congress."

George Bush [Sr.]

"I'm not a member of any organized political

party, I'm a Democrat."
Will Rogers

Nothing is certain, but death and taxes
*

Taxes – What government takes from the people, but
returns later, less a handling fee
*

Self praise is no recommendation
*

Three may keep a secret, if two of them are dead
*

**"You can't depend on the man who made the mess
to clean it up."**
Richard Nixon
*

Every man has his price
*

"If I were two faced, would I be wearing this one?"
Abraham Lincoln
*

You can't fight City Hall
*

**"Ask not what your country can do for you. Ask
what you can do for your country."**
John F. Kennedy

*

**"A diplomat is a man who always remembers a
woman's birthday, but never remembers her age."**
Robert Frost
*

Men have become tools of their tools
*

If you have never contemplated how large a
billion is, here is something to compare it to.

A billion seconds ago was 1960
and
A billion minutes ago Jesus was alive
*

To a politician, a billion must seem like a.....

Drop in the bucket

because our government spends one every 8 ½ hours
and
our national deficit approaches a trillion dollars
but
That's another story
*

A skeleton in every family's closet.

GUESTS

Fish, like guests, begin to smell after three days

In my opinion, one could reduce that time to after one evening or at most one day. No, seriously, I don't have a problem with having guests over. I will have to admit that I once learned a lesson from a very bad experience relating to guests.

My second wife's sister, who was a divorced mother with two kids, lived about a mile from us. She was a nice, attractive, petite, young woman. I say was, because I haven't seen her for about twenty years, so she isn't too young any more and physical characteristics do change over time, unfortunately.

She became involved with a loser, in my opinion, who talked her into selling her home, buying a camping trailer, marrying him, and taking off to live on the road like gypsies. I'll call them Jack and Jill, because I don't remember their names.

Jack was unemployed at the time and my ex-wife told me that he did not work very often after his marriage to Jill. They evidently lived off the proceeds from the house sale. By the way, I do remember my X's name, but I choose not to use it. I didn't want to appear senile, although a failing memory may be the first indication, but I do forget names easily.

About a year later, my X told me her sister and family were going to be driving through the area and wanted to stay at the camp for awhile to visit. I didn't see anything wrong with them staying over.

They arrived in mid June, with the same old camper, which they hooked up to electricity from my workshop. After a few days, I was informed that their air conditioner was not working properly and the four of them were going to be staying inside with us. At the time we lived in a single wide mobile home with two bedrooms. Space was already at a premium. How would you take it in my situation?

This arrangement went on for days and I began to get very irritated about the whole deal. I was particularly upset when I came in from work and there was no place to sit, because Jack's relatives had come over to visit them, instead of the other way around. My X told me that Jack couldn't afford gas to drive around and visit his relation. A big red flag began to fly after hearing that info. If he could not afford fuel to visit, how could he afford to leave?

Summer camp was almost over and we had plans to head out to Colorado for my long awaited summer vacation. I told my X that the guests would have to leave very soon, because they could not be there while we were gone. She told me that she was going to stay at home with them. I was remarkably calm about the news.

My vacation began and I left with my dog, instead of my wife. The affair was......

The straw that broke the camel's back

I realized as I drove out the gate that our marriage was over. Black and I spent a splendid two weeks camping in the majestic mountains of central Colorado. The day after I returned, I went to my lawyer and filed for divorce. I never regretted my decision, but she did, for she told me several years later that she had blown it. I asked her, "Why?" She told me that she just wanted to piss me off. She had accomplished her goal.

"Some cause happiness wherever they go; others whenever they go."

Oscar Wilde

*

You are what you eat.

HEALTH

An apple a day keeps the doctor away

I felt it fitting to begin with probably the most popular saying that even the very young have heard. Could it be that Johnny Appleseed started this one to boost sales?

*

Early to bed and early to rise, makes one healthy, wealthy, and wise

OK, that one is cute and catchy, but I would certainly not bank on it. As I have gotten older, it seems that I go to bed earlier and earlier, but I can't say I'm wiser. As a matter of fact, last night I told Lynda I was going to bed. She informed me it was only 8:00 p.m., so I reluctantly decided to stay up longer. I returned to the computer room to write more and managed to postpone bedtime until a little after nine. I do get up early, but I see no direct correlation of proof to back up the saying.

*

Six hours sleep for a man, seven for a woman, and

Ray Racobs

eight for a fool

The only time I can remember sleeping over eight hours was back in the days when I was drinking and had a hangover. I **was** a fool then.

*

One hours sleep before midnight is worth two after

*

He lives long who lives well

*

35 is when you finally get your head together and your body starts falling apart

*

What we need to fear is fear itself

If you believe all the results from all of the studies that have cost us taxpayers billions of dollars then you can understand that.....

[All we have to fear is everything we eat, drink, or come in contact with.]

*

There is a remedy for everything, but death

*

Eat to live, don't live to eat

*

MOST IRRITATING NOISE # 6

The sound of someone getting sick, even in a movie, almost makes me sick. The sight of it is even worse.

A man is as old as he feels, but a woman is as old as

she looks

That may explain why the contents of my medicine cabinet consist of items like Ben Gay, Alka Seltzer, Excedrin, etc., and Lynda's is stuffed full of cosmetics and skin care products.

*

It is not work that kills, but worry

My main worry would have to be about the future, when I decide to retire. Will I have enough income from my retirement, social security, IRA, and TDA to enjoy those final years? At least I will have some forms of income that many do not have. It is better to be concerned about things rather than worry about them. Worry is stressful.

Couples who are about the same age and are drawing only social security have got to be having a tough time financially. The difference between Lynda's age and mine is one advantage that we have, which was not intentional. She could still be earning a decent wage from teaching for several years after I retire. This would help ease us into the world of being senior citizens.

*

A trouble shared, is a trouble halved

*

No pain, no gain

*

You are what you eat

I have never heard of the saying "You are what you drink", which may be good. Years ago I may have turned into a beer can. Today, I could be walking around looking like a coffee can. I drink way too much coffee and I know it, but it really gets me going in the morning. I don't know what my excuse is in the afternoon. I do have to be careful and not consume the beverage into the evening or I will not sleep well. I know people who drink coffee in the late evening and have no problem.

*

Just what the doctor ordered

*

Feed a cold and starve a fever

*

Prevention is better than cure

*

Laughter is the best medicine

*

It runs in the family

*

HOME

It is only fitting to begin with…..

Home is where the heart is
*
Charity begins at home

[Charity is beginning to take a toll on my wallet.]
*
A place for everything and everything in its place

      Lynda's idea of how a home should be kept differs somewhat from my view.   My place for many things does not quite correspond to her idea of a proper place. I think the back of a few chairs is a good location to hang clothes I have worn, but are not dirty enough, in my view, to be washed. It's not like I put my clothes on all the chairs. I always make sure there are a few available for us to use for sitting.

The wife is the key to the house

We discussed the matter the other evening. I explained the reasoning behind my actions, but Lynda didn't seem to understand my point of view. She told me to, "Hang them back up or put them in the dirty clothes hamper." Well, I responded with something that must have been offensive, because I had to make my own supper again. I still say.....

Any excuse is better than no excuse
*

Home away from home
*

Those who live in glass houses, shouldn't throw stones

[Those who live in glass houses should invest heavily in curtains]
*

Keep a thing for seven years and you'll find a use for it

[Keep a thing for seven years and you'll need a bigger house in five]
*

You've made your bed, now lie in it

[You've made your bed, now take out the trash]
*

If you can't stand the heat, get out of the kitchen

[If you can't stand the heat, turn on the AC]

MOST IRRITATING NOISE # 7

Lynda goes through the house and vacuums each Saturday. I can't concentrate on anything while she is cleaning.

*

PERSONAL FACT

For a brief time (fortunately) in my life, I had no place to call home and lived out of my car. It was not a very big car, either. I really do give thanks for having a nice home to live in and I do like the way that Lynda keeps the house. I promise to make an effort to pick up after myself.

The size or grandeur of the home does not matter, but a nice home should be a place of comfort and tranquility. A home is even more valued when someone special is there to share it with. I am truly blessed.

*

Rules are made to be broken.

LAW

"Vote early and vote often"
Al Capone

*

A man who is his own lawyer has a fool for a client

*

Ignorance of the law is no excuse for breaking it

*

Crime doesn't pay

*

"Associate yourself with men of good quality...for 'tis better to be alone than in bad company."
George Washington

*

A man is known by the company he keeps

*

Guilt by association

*

"I tried to walk a line between acting lawfully and testifying falsely, but I now realize that I did not fully accomplish that goal."
Bill Clinton

*

One law for the rich and another for the poor

*

Possession is 9/10ths of the law

It is the other 1/10th that will get you into trouble for possessing something that isn't yours.

*

Finders keepers, losers weepers

*

"An unjust law is no law at all."
Saint Augustine

*

Hang a thief when he's young and he won't steal when he's old

*

When accused of anything, deny everything

*

"Denial ain't just a river in Egypt."
Mark Twain

*

Two wrongs don't make a right

For you math wizards, though, a negative times a negative does make a positive, somehow.

Eye for an eye.

Let the punishment fit the crime
*

Rules were made to be broken

I was pulled over for speeding once very late at night, or very early in the morning, to be more precise. The officer and I exchanged pleasantries and he asked why I was speeding. I responded with….. "I was going with the flow of traffic." He told me that I was the only one on the road. I replied with confidence ….."Exactly, I was the flow." I must have caught him in a good mood, because he laughed and told me to "Slow down and get out of here." I would not guarantee that response to work very often.
*

There is an exception to every rule
*

Not worth the paper it's written on
*

The ends justify the means

and the reverse…..

The ends don't always justify the means

*

Liars should have good memories.

LIES and DECEIT

A liar ought to have a good memory
*

There was a span of about fifteen years when I was not particularly truthful in all of what I said to others. From my late teens, until I was thirty-three, my lies were frequent.

During my younger days, prior to graduating from high school, I was not very popular. This was due to a series of factors, which I had little control over. Through my high school years, my family lived in three different school districts. I was always the "new" kid and never seemed to mix in well. The relocation also separated me from any friends that I had made.

When I first went to college, I was a freed person. I wanted to be popular. I wanted to become somebody. No one knew me or anything about me. I could tell anyone anything and they would not know any different. I succeeded, but there were drawbacks. Lying had become a habit. Over the years, there were times when I really thought some lies were real.

I finally faced reality at the treatment center mentioned in the next chapter. Even though I had entered voluntarily, I was their "guest" for a month.

We were forced to adhere to a rigid schedule of classes, group sessions, and other meetings.

While learning about the Ten Step Program, I was able to evaluate myself as a person and could admit I was wrong. I was a finally successful at something. I don't know if I was truly "reborn" in the religious sense, but I was a new and improved person inside. I found out a few years later that there were only two of us, out of about thirty in my "class", who had not returned to drinking.

It is ironic, in a way, but I detest being lied to and when it occurs, I take the intentional inaccuracy personal. In one way or another, a lie is an insult to ones intelligence.

*

My previous two marriages ended primarily because of lies and deceit. I will accept most of the blame for the first one, but very little for the second breakup. I married both times for the wrong reason, but I am not writing a tell-all manual on how to stay married. I am just letting you know that in marriage and life in general.....

Honesty is the best policy

Promises, like pie crust, are meant to be broken
*
I wasn't born yesterday

Even if I was born yesterday, I wouldn't believe you.
*
The best way to keep one's word is not to give it

*

There are two sides to every story

On occasion I have watched one of those court room shows where, I assume, a former judge hears short civil disputes and comes up with a verdict that is binding on all parties. In virtually all of the cases I have seen one side will refute most of the other side's story. Someone is obviously lying. I usually pick the opposite one for whom "Judge Judy" has ruled in favor of.

*

A liar is not believed when he tells the truth

Think back when you were a kid and recall the "Chicken Little" story about the sky is falling. By the way, the story is still read in schools today.

*

Believe nothing of what you hear and only half of what you see

So much for.....

What everyone says, must be true

and.....

Seeing is believing

At a magic show, what you see is seldom what you really see.

*

Now you see it, now you don't

*

Opportunity knocks only once.

LIFE IN GENERAL

Life begins at forty

[Life begins at forty, if you are forty]
*

Forty is the old age of youth and fifty is the youth of old age

Whew! I felt a lot better after hearing about that one from one of my older friends. I need to find one that will make me more at ease when sixty rolls around, because I often seem to be falling into the mold of the next familiar proverb.

You are only as old as you feel
*
You win a few, you lose a few
*
Don't drink and drive

I was being truthful when I said I learned how to drink when I went to Kansas State University, after high school in 1964. I didn't drive while I was there, which was a good thing. I probably would not be here today if I had.

I could probably write an entire book just about the exploits in my life that dealt with alcohol consumption. Let me say this. Drinking became pretty much a priority to my existence after dropping out of college. I never went anywhere if beer or booze was not allowed. I never drank on the job, but I often had an iced down six pack waiting for me in the car. The supply in the parking lot allowed me to get home, feed the dog, and head to my favorite tavern, where of course, I would stay until closing time.

After my discharge from the U. S. Navy, I bought a new '69 Javelin. I finally had to retire it, due to a major collision, seven years later. Even before that accident, the poor vehicle looked like I had entered it in a weekly demolition derby.

Finally, after over thirteen years, I got sick and tired of being sick and tired. I checked myself into an alcohol treatment center on December 7, 1977. I immediately became quite familiar with AA's most popular saying.

One day at a time

I have remained, not only sober since then, but have never taken one sip of beer, wine, or hard stuff, since that day. The anniversary of the bombing of Pearl Harbor in 1941 is also my anniversary. It's ironic, in a way, that Hawaii got bombed on that day and I didn't.

It was not only fortunate for me to quit drinking, but probably lucky for others as well. In the time frame of my being *off the wagon*, I was, by law, driving drunk for a total of about 3,285 days. I am very thankful that my poor choices, early in life, did not result in someone losing their life. I recall a statistic that estimates up to 60 % of all fatalities in vehicle accidents have been drug and/or alcohol related.

The only ticket I received, while under the influence, was for driving an unsafe vehicle. I was pulled over by an officer, who had seen my passenger door fly open. The door would not latch, due to an earlier wreck, so I had it wired shut, but the wire broke in front of the cop. When I look back, I am amazed with all that I got away with. I was either very lucky or somehow blessed.

After I achieved sobriety status, I attended a few AA meetings at various sites in Salina, but I did not really like them. The majority of the talk among the folks there pertained to how much fun they had while drinking. Although probably true, it seemed a little counter productive to me. The fun I have now, being sober, is much more meaningful and chances are I'll remember it the next day.

Better to be envied than pitied
*
To error is human, to forgive divine
*
Better to be safe than sorry

Appearances can be deceiving with.....

All that glitters is not gold
and
Beauty is only skin deep
*

I'd rather be lucky than good

[I'd rather be lucky than unlucky]
*

I wasn't born yesterday

[Even if I was born yesterday, I wouldn't believe you]
*

***If a thing is worth doing, it is worth doing well the
first time***
*

If you want something done right, do it yourself

On second thought, you had better pay a professional
to do it.
*

Make haste slowly
*

Haste makes waste
*

Seek and ye shall find

[Seek and you will find many things that you had
previously lost.]

Thought is free

Second thoughts are best

Long line – If one is unable to carry on a normal conversation with the individual who is at the front of the line, then it is a long line.

I detest waiting in lines for almost any reason. It doesn't matter if it is a line of traffic or a line of shopping carts at the store. I feel that the wait is wasting part of my life away.

When I am by myself the feeling is even worse. I need to figure out something constructive to do while standing in line. I'll mull that one over.

*

He who hesitates is lost

[He who hesitates, gets there later]

*

I have a wonderful line that I use anytime that I am late to anything, for any reason. I don't waste time thinking up something that sounds believable.

I don't even give the actual reason or true excuse
of why I was late. I simply say "I'd have been here
sooner, if I'd have left sooner." That covers it all. It
is really a ***no brainer*** and it really surprises those who
I say it to. I honestly have to say that I have never
heard anyone use it before. Well, I give you my full
permission to borrow it.

*

The best things in life are free

*

Free – Things of no value.

*

Waste not, want not

*

Dead men tell no tales

That was before "CSI" and "CSI Miami" depicted the
use of modern forensic medicine.

*

No news is good news

*

Bad news travels fast

Is there a good time to give bad news to a
member of the family? I say no, but there are most
certainly bad or at least inappropriate times to notify
someone of bad news. I won't go into specifics, but
I received a long distance call, in the middle of the
night, with some bad news. At 2:00 A.M. there was
nothing I could do about the situation. Even though
I tried, I could not get back to sleep. That day was
bad enough to begin with, but now I had to deal with

stress along with the fatigue from little sleep. If you ever have to be the bearer of bad news use some judgment as to the best time to give it.

*

Anything is easier to get into than out of
*
It is a sad heart that never rejoices
*
There is safety in numbers
*
The more the merrier

When I used to drink and party, I would have agreed with the previous entry. I am much older, a lot wiser, more reserved, and less inclined to be the life of the party. I am not always comfortable at large family functions or other gatherings in confined places. Eventually I get very tired of the noise and must leave.

*

Misery loves company
*
One good turn deserves another
*
If you play with fire you will get burnt
*
Fight fire with fire

The bigger they are, the harder they fall

[The bigger they are, the harder they will kick your butt]

*

There's no use crying over spilt milk

What if it was chocolate milk and you spilt it on your new $200 cashmere sweater?

It will all come out in the wash
*
What's done is done
*
That's the way it is

If a person does not have the guts or gumption to say something about the way things are, it will more than likely stay that way.
*

Life is no bed of roses

It is if they are not the thorn less variety.
*

It too shall pass
*
Ask not, want not
*

I've got a tip for you. Have you ever thought about complaining to your spouse about any of her relatives? Don't because…..

Blood is thicker than water
*
What you don't know can't hurt you
*

He who laughs last laughs best (or longest)
*

It is never too late to mend your pants

It is, if you forgot and wore them to work yesterday.
*

First come, first served
*

Better late than never

It may even, at times, be appropriate in reverse.

Better never than late

That would be my philosophy on arriving too late for the beginning of a movie. If Lynda and I are running behind schedule to get to the cinema on time, I would rather not go. It's O. K. to miss the previews and we can always go back for popcorn and drinks, but they won't restart the flick.
*

Don't get mad, get even
*

Don't judge a book by its cover
or
You can't tell a book by its cover

At this time, I haven't prepared the front cover for the book. I want it to be distinctive and appealing to make people want to look at it. By the way, to do the back cover will cost me a hundred big ones extra, so I hope it will be an eye catcher as well.

*

Good riddance to bad rubbish
*

***Fool me once, shame on you,
fool me twice shame on me***
*

Don't make the same mistake twice
*

Don't let the door kick you in the butt
*

All good things come to those who wait

Like a bus or cab in a rainstorm?

The previous saying implies that we should be patient. I took an informal survey from a few people that I spoke with while pondering the statement. I heard things like; Christmas, Fridays, weekends, paydays, store sales, holidays, weddings, kids, tax refunds, and even old age. I guess.....

Patience is a virtue

Things will happen and they will come, so don't worry about them. Don't get patience confused with procrastination. There is a thin line between waiting and doing.
*

Procrastination is the thief of time
*

The opposite of life is obviously death. When others die before their time, I am saddened. It is a pity, but we have little control over when we depart.

I have only been to four funerals. The first funeral was for my father. I did not care for any part of the whole affair. I would have sworn never to attend another funeral, but I knew there would be others. I certainly haven't gone out of my way to take part in the ritual.

Lynda has informed me that funerals are for the living. It is a time to honor those who have left us and also a time to console those who remain. I agree with the principle. It is not that I am not a sympathetic and caring person. Maybe it's due to the fact that I am selfish and don't want to deal with the misery. I will make an effort to forgo my personal feelings and resign to the fact that we often must do some things in life that are unpleasant.

I recently went to the funeral of a long time friend, but hadn't attended one for a number of years. Protocol must have changed. From the looks of the participants at the affair, I would not have thought it was a funeral. Black was not the prevalent color and jeans are apparently not taboo these days. Lynda was surprised to hear that I had only been to three other funerals. It was the third one she had attended within the past year.

Life goes on

*

Gone, but not forgotten

*

Life's not all what it's cracked up to be

To me, it beats the heck out of the alternative

*

Live every day as if it were your last

I think we had better not do that in the literal sense. If I knew today was to be my last I certainly would not show up for work and I would throw a heck of a party.

*

The best is yet to come

*

Love at first sight.

LOVE

It is better to have loved and lost, than never to have loved at all

    This was probably meant to comfort or console one who had broken up with their bow, significant other, or spouse. It could also be used to rationalize the fact that you have been dumped for another.

*

Absence makes the heart grow fonder

    Does it? What about.....

Out of sight, out of mind

    Yes, you aren't the only one who has lost their "true love" to another. Many of us have been members to that club at least once and more than once wouldn't be unusual.

*

If you are thinking about being unfaithful to the one you "love", remember that…..

What's good for the gander is good for the goose
What comes around goes around
or is it…..
What goes around comes around
*

Whatever you do, if you are a guy, don't forget…..

Hell hath no fury like a woman scorned
*
All's fair in love and war
and…..
Variety is the spice of life

I hope you don't believe or follow either of those, because doing so could make you part of the statistic that 50% of marriages end in divorce.
*
It takes two to quarrel
*
Opposites attract

I am not sold on the idea that opposites make good matches though.
*
Two's company, three's a crowd
*
Never say never
*
A good Jack makes a good Jill

*

Honor thy Father and Mother
*

If at first you don't succeed, try, try again

This would imply that one will fail more than once at any particular endeavor. I placed it under this chapter, since it is personally applicable. I have been married three times and it was fitting in my case that…..

The third time is the charm
*

So don't get down on yourself if you fail at romance or marriage, because…..

There are plenty more fish in the sea.
*

You can't lose what you never had
*

I have been out of the dating routine for a bunch of years, but I remember these next words well. I will admit to uttering the words myself. Both sexes have used it, for a variety of reasons, probably ever since the invention of the telephone.

I'll call you
*

Love is never having to say you are sorry
*

Never, like always, is a long time
*

Love is blind
*

Love at first sight

I don't scoff at those who have uttered those words, because it happened to me **once** and luckily, I married her.

One of my duties, as a Camp Ranger, is to check groups in who use the site. I was doing just that when a van came through the entry gate and pulled up near my truck. I walked over to the vehicle and saw Lynda. I was so taken by her beauty that I could hardly accomplish the check in procedures. I took more time, on purpose, because I didn't want her to drive off.

I was **on cloud nine,** as they say, and I came up with lame excuses to visit the cabin, where Lynda and her Girl Scout troop was staying, just to see her again. I was disappointed, the next day, when I had to check her troop out, since she would be leaving.

That was the first time that her troop had been to Camp Seikooc. For several years I had the good fortune to see Lynda fairly often at Girl Scout functions or when one of her two troops would return to camp. As time went by, Lynda eventually separated and later obtained a divorce. Within two years after her breakup, we were married.

Behind every great man, there is a woman

One evening, years later, we met Jess and his wife, Linda, for dinner. Jess had been my supervisor when I first met "my" Lynda. In our idle chit chat Jess, for some reason, began a story about when we worked together. He recounted how I came up to him and blurted out, "I met the most beautiful woman in the world over the weekend". I did recall the incident, but had never told Lynda about it. She was pleased. I will never forget our first encounter. It changed my life forever, for the better.

*

When poverty comes in the door, love flies out the window

If that should happen to you, it wasn't true love anyway, since someone did not take their vows, "for better or worse, for richer or poorer", seriously.

*

It takes a loose rein to keep a horse tight and a marriage right

A good sense of humor and a willingness to compromise doesn't hurt either.

*

Lynda and I got married on May 25, 1994, outside of Breckenridge, Colorado. I don't know how we came up with the area, since there are so many other places in Colorado that we enjoy. We had only been to Breckenridge once before. The minister was from Frisco, CO, and we enlisted him sight unseen, over the phone.

He told us he and his wife had exchanged their vows at a scenic overlook north of town called Sapphire Point. We said the location sounded great to us and we set the date. We made reservations at a nice ski resort and drove out to the area a couple of days before the event. It would be small in size, but huge in meaning.

On the eve of our ceremony we were having lunch at a quaint little outdoor café. Sitting near us were two young women. I overheard one talking about taking pictures. Lynda and I had not even mentioned picture taking of the wedding. We broke into their conversation and told them of our plans for the next day. Neither of them was busy and we "signed them up". They took photos and also serveed as our witnesses. It was a stroke of luck, I suppose.

Everything went together smoothly, as if we had planned it for weeks. Lynda had a portable music player with several tapes to be played at different times. The girl not taking the still shots ran the music and video taped the ceremony. We were going to have the camcorder on a tripod, but this worked out much better. We even had guests. A few resident chipmunks and ground squirrels scurried around on the ground and stone retaining wall with great excitement over the event.

Our wedding was like none other that I had ever been to or heard of. It was free from all of the hoopla and festivities. We didn't send out hundreds of invitations. We hadn't rented an expensive place to have the reception. We had no entourage of all the bridesmaids and groomsmen who have nothing to do anyway, but stand around. We had been able to forgo the lengthy, laborious, and boring process of picture taking after the wedding. We simply got married and it was all so wonderful.

That night we changed rooms at the Inn and stayed in one of their sweets. It was lovely. The management had even set out a very nice fruit basket centerpiece on the dining room table for us. There was a private hot tub in the room and a fireplace. We utilized both of them pleasurably that night.

Lynda's parents had planned a reception for us at their house upon our return home. We had a big cook out and it was quite enjoyable. All of the major headaches and financial nightmares associated with

any big wedding had been eliminated. Our wedding
and honeymoon cost us about six hundred dollars.

Both of Lynda's daughters are getting married
this summer. I am really concerned about the costs
that we will have to bear. Neither of them are being
what I would call frugal over expenses. I understand
that weddings are expensive, but when I overhear
some of the expenses involved I can hardly believe
my ears. I have tried very hard for several years to
get our spending under control and lowering our
debts. This year, for me anyway, will be a financially
depressing one.

*

What's mine is hers, what's hers is hers

*

Cold hands, warm heart

[If you have cold hands you should wear gloves]

What part of the anatomy is warm, if one has
cold feet? We've heard about someone getting cold
feet and not going through with their plans.

*

Good things come in threes.

MISCELLANEOUS

Fact is stranger than fiction

This was, of course, said before Stephen Spielberg, J. K. Rowling, and J.R.R. Tolkien wrote and published novels.

*

Gay - It used to mean happy

*

There is a time and place for everything

*

Tools – Things borrowed from Dad that are not put back or not returned at all

*

Accidents will (do) happen

*

Small is beautiful

*

Thank God it's Friday

There are an awfully lot of people out there, including Lynda, who utter those words every Friday. My weekly work schedule is somewhat different than most, in that my days off are during the week. The bulk of the non-summer camp usage occurs over the weekends. My Sunday is other people's Friday.

*

Rome was not built in a day

Really, well imagine that!

*

Be careful for what you wish for; you may get it

*

I have a favorite number, as most of us do. It is 231. It didn't start out being my favorite number, it just happened one day. In 1964, my dorm room at college was, you guessed it, 231. That would have been the end of the story, but that number came back after thirty years of meaning nothing to me.

Lynda and I went to a bed and breakfast, in Guthrie, Oklahoma, in 1995, for our first wedding anniversary. Our room number was, you guessed it again, 231. Ever since then the number just keeps showing up. I will wake up in the middle of the night, often at 2:31 a.m. When we go on trips out of town, invariably I will suddenly see a 231 highway mile marker. It's not like I look at each mile marker, just waiting for the number to come up, either. Part of our trips through Colorado are on Colorado Hwy 231.

On one Colorado trip, we went to cash a traveler's check at a small bank in Lake City, Colorado. The bank's address was 231 Silver Street. I immediately opened up a savings account. Why? I don't know why. It has become really weird and almost eerie, at times.

My book has been given a tracking number and it begins with 231. Grizzly's This'N That will have 231 numbered pages, but that was by design.

*

Look before you leap

[Look before you walk across a cow lot]
*

It's like looking for a needle in a hay stack

As most of you know, in colder weather a person's fingers will shrink. So do other parts of some people's anatomy, but I won't .....

Touch that one with a ten foot pole
*

At any rate, Lynda bought me a very special (and expensive) ring as a college graduation gift. Since it was a surprise gift, she didn't know what size to have it made. It was just a tad bit loose, but close enough.

One of my daily chores, when we had our horses, was to feed them grain and hay. I was at the barn doing those tasks last December, when the ring came off as I threw a bale of hay into the horse lot. The time of day complicated my retrieval of the ring, because it was early evening and darkness had set in. I looked for it as best as I could, with no positive results. I put the horses in a side pen and fed them again.

I returned the next morning at first light to continue the search, but didn't fair any better. I finally called a local hardware store that sold metal detectors. They knew of a gentleman who, for a fee, would come out with his detector and search for lost items. I called him and told him the situation. He was out within an hour and I showed him the area where I suspected the ring was. Remarkably, he found it within a minute after he began. It was surely the quickest $50 the guy had ever made, but I was elated. I may never have found it, since one of the horses had obviously stepped on it, for the ring was buried three inches under the ground.

Give me a break

You would think that I had learned a lesson, but I didn't. I lost it this winter when throwing straw into my large, special built, 4x4x8 foot, dog house. Fortunately, I knew the ring was within the confines of the dog house. I took almost all of the straw out, a handful at a time, before I found it. I have, I believe, now learned my lesson. If it happens again, I will not tell anyone.

*

X-Ray - Someone named "Ray", who changed his name

*

A penny for your thoughts.

MONEY

A rich man has ice in the summer, while the poor man must wait 'till winter
*
Money is the root of all evil
*
Money is power
*

Gratuity or tip – Money expected at most eating establishments, in addition to the cost of the meal, for service, which may or may not have been good.

I don't follow the unwritten rule or guideline for tipping at restaurants, which usually goes directly to the person who waited on my table. The normal amount of the tip used to be 10% of the total food bill, but evidently it is now at 15%. For some maybe.

At some businesses, a gratuity of 15% is automatically added to one's bill, which, in my opinion, is not right. In fact, I don't think the amount of the tip should be based on the food bill at all and I will give you a very simple example of why.

Let's say that my wife and I went out to eat at the same restaurant for dinner three nights in a row. On the first night we had pasta meals. On the second night we had chicken plates and on the third night we had steak. The bill for each meal was $14, $18, and $24 respectively. Therefore the tips, under the "rules" for tipping would have been $2.10, $2.70, and $3.60. The service was probably no different for each of the meals, but the tip expected increased. Now, to me, there is something wrong with that picture. When Lynda and I go out to eat, I will leave at least a $2 or $3 tip irregardless of the price of the meals. I will leave more if the service is extra good.

*

Poverty is no disgrace, but it is a great inconvenience

*

Money talks louder than words

*

Money isn't everything

Really…..whoever spoke those words must have been broke.

*

Easy come, easy go

*

A picture is worth a thousand words

[A picture is worth a thousand dollars, if it can be sold for a profit.]

*

Take care of the pence (pennies) and the pounds

(dollars) **will take care of themselves**
*

"A penny saved, is a penny earned."
Ben Franklin

[A penny saved earns little interest]
*
A penny for your thoughts

There are a lot of times when I would have been glad to give someone much more than a penny to know what they were thinking.
*

"If you can count your money, you aren't a billionaire."
J. Paul Getty
*

A fool and his money are soon parted
*

Don't take any wooden nickels
*

Nothing ventured, nothing gained
*

Save for a rainy day
*

Pay me now or pay me later

[Pay me now, I can't wait till later]
*
The rich get richer and the poor get poorer

**If you save when you are young, you can spend
when you are old**
*

Lottery – A payment of money in exchange for a
chance of riches

Jess Maus, a good friend and former boss
of mine, described the lottery as not being a waste
of money for most people, because it gave them a
moment to dream. I would have to agree with him. I
fork over a few bucks a week in hopes of becoming
rich. I heard a joke that described buying lottery
tickets as a "rednecks retirement plan".

A few months ago the value of the Power
Ball Lottery in our area was over 200 million dollars.
Lynda and I decided to sit down and make a list of
what each of us would do, if we were lucky and won
that much money. We compared our lists and were
surprised with the similarities.

Our close relatives, who don't play, should
hope and pray that I win a fortune. All of them will
be well taken care of if I do win millions. My plan
dictates that all their bills will be paid, college trust
funds will be set up for the kids, and a sizeable chunk
of cash will be given to each of them directly.
*

Another day, another dollar

A day late and a dollar short
*

170

Rob Peter to pay Paul

I don't do the above, but I certainly transfer credit card balances back and forth to obtain a lower interest rate. I have at least been able to eliminate all cards with a double digit rate.

*

Cheats never prosper
*

Money doesn't grow on trees
*

That will cost you an arm and a leg
*

The grass is always greener.

NATURE

The grass is always greener on the other side of the fence

[The grass is always greener, if it is watered regularly]

*

Lightening never strikes in the same place twice

I know for a fact that, even though rare, it does happen. I have had evidence of it at Camp Seikooc. In the '60's a young adult was killed by lightening. A maple tree was planted in her memory near the site of the accident. During my tenure, the tree was fully mature and about 60 feet tall. It was struck twice by lightening.

I have also spoken to an area farmer, who informed me that he has lost three cows due to lightening strikes in the same place, under a large elm tree in his pasture.

*

"What's in a name? A rose by any other name would smell as sweet."

William Shakespeare

*

Some can't see the forest because of the trees

My exposure to the Colorado Rockies and other western areas of the state came in the early seventies during deer hunting trips. The first time I went was with five of my drinking buddies. It would be the first of several annual pilgrimages. We did more partying than hunting, but actually did come home each year loaded with iced down venison. Before my first trip out, I had never shot a deer or even shot at deer before. Incidentally, I still haven't.

On that first trip, we had driven overnight from Salina, KS, so we could set up our camp during the daylight hours. The season opened the next day, but we had time to check out where we had planned to hunt. The area was like a scene from a western movie. It consisted of several massive valleys leading up into forests.

We drew straws to pick hunting partners. On the first morning out, I was with Gary Diehl, who was an experienced hunter. He had never shot a deer

174

before either. We took one of the vehicles and drove
a few miles from our campsite to a spot overlooking
a stand of timber. We got out and slowly walked
around the rim of woods. After about an hour into the
hike, Gary motioned to me to stop. I saw him level
his rifle, aim, and fire. The blast startled me and the
sound echoed down the valley. He had dropped a 10
point buck. We field dressed it with jubilation and
started to drag the carcass uphill, around huge rocks,
and through trees. The buck, before it expired, had
managed to travel several hundred feet below from
where it was hit. The task was awful. We were not
acclimated to the altitude and could only manage a
few feet at a time before we had to rest and catch our
breaths. I never will forget how exhausting the chore
was. I thought my heart and lungs would burst.

      For the rest of that trip and two others, I had
nice "trophy" bucks in my sights, but I never pulled
the trigger. I always thought of an excuse not to
fire. The excursions did make me realize that I loved
the majestic mountains, the magnificent scenery, the
abundant wild life, and the smell of the crisp clear air.
I love seeing deer on our trips to the mountains, but
now I only take pictures of them.

A thing of beauty is a joy forever

Ray Racobs

*

I have hesitated putting this portion about our favorite picnic area into the book. There may be a number of people at Blue Mesa who may like to buy a copy of it and the "secret" would be out. It's not really a secret, but there has rarely been anyone at the small lake when we have driven up for the afternoon.

Just west of Blue Mesa Ranch a narrow, unmarked, dirt road leaves the highway, heads north across a cattle guard, and goes up into the hills. After about eight miles it becomes more scenic with steeper valleys and more trees. The spot is just over thirteen miles from the highway and is named Rainbow Lake.

There are a number of different hiking trails leading around, above, and away from the lake. Our stays at Blue Mesa will always include a pleasant and relaxing trip to Rainbow Lake.

*

You can take the boy out of the country, but you can't take the country our of the boy

*

Plant oak trees now for your heirs later

*

A short time after President John F. Kennedy was assassinated, an open field at Camp Seikooc was named "Kennedy Meadow". The Girl Scouts planted an Austrian Pine in the center of the field, in his memory. The tree was only about eight feet tall when I came there in 1980, partly because it had no central leader for height. The width of the tree was normal for its age. One of the shots fired that fateful day hit President Kennedy in the head. No other limbs on the tree ever took over to become the top of the tree, as would normally happen in nature.

*

In the past, as a newcomer to the world of the forests in Colorado, I have done some pretty dumb things. A few of my errors in judgment or from the lack of experience could have cost me dearly. I will include a few stories to keep others out of trouble.

I once saw a huge hornets nest (the kind that looks like a football) hanging from a tree limb only about ten feet off the ground. I saw no hornet activity whatsoever around the nest or tree. I tried to climb the tree, but I was not agile enough to shimmy up it. I soon found a branch on the ground that was long enough to dislodge if from the limb. When I began to move the nest back and forth with the branch something unforeseen happened.......the hornets came pouring out. I am allergic to wasp stings and I was miles from any medical help, but here I was screwing around with a hornets nest. I was very lucky. I ran well enough to get away from them.

*

I have been on float trips on numerous rivers in Colorado with ratings of I (mild) to IV (wild), but haven't thought that at one moment a river could be quite tame and later be quite dangerous.

I had been hiking along a section of the Pewter River and decided to wade across and hike in the hills beyond. On my trip across, the water was at my knees. I was away for several hours and returned to the same spot where I had originally crossed. I went a few feet into the water and became confused. The water was about six inches over my knees. I looked around and saw landmarks that proved I was at the same spot on the river. I waded on and the water was at my hips when I was swept off my feet. With backpack and other assorted gear it was quite difficult to swim laterally towards the other bank, but I was able to get a foot hold after traveling about a hundred yards or so down stream. Evidently a storm had occurred up stream and the water volume had raised the height of the river. It wasn't too smart to cross the way I had. In the future I won't cross any major water ways without a bridge handy.

While on the subject of water, a hike to a place called Crater Lake comes to mind. Walking along a stream has a soothing effect on the mind. This is why people buy those little water falls for their home or back yard patio.

I followed the trail for over a mile along side a fair sized stream. The trail led to the streams edge and then across some large rocks to the other side. It was just before I began to cross over when I saw them.....bear tracks. I froze. I squatted down for a better look, and felt very, very peculiar. Have you ever had that eerie feeling that you were being watched? That is how I felt at that time. I slowly looked left and right to view what I could in the thick woodland. I looked again at the tracks to see if I could tell where they led. The tracks in view did look as if they were going the same way I was headed.

By feeling the edges of the tracks I could tell they were fresh. They were as wide as my hand and I have a pretty good sized hand. I must have crouched there for fifteen minutes just looking around. I was actually spooked. I finally stood up, gingerly turned around and returned to the trailhead, but this time, a good hundred feet from the water's edge. The sound of the water had obviously been louder than my bell. I couldn't tell you how many times I looked over my shoulder on the way back.

*

Let nature take its course

Two heads are better than one.

PEOPLE

It takes all kinds of people to make a world
You can fool some of the people all of the time, all of
the people some of the time, but you can't fool all of
the people all of the time
*

I went to New York once for a week long
training seminar. One day we had an afternoon off
and four of us guys decided to go into the "City"
for some sightseeing. We rode a train into Grand
Central Station and took a subway from there to "who
knows where". We all lived in the Midwest and were
experiencing the "Big Apple" for the first time. We
had noticed the people did not particularly want to
talk to us, much less make eye contact.

Don't stick your neck out

We were standing on a corner and I told the
others to follow my lead. I pointed to the sky and the
others did the same. I was watching people as they
walked past......you could tell that they wanted to
look up, but just couldn't force their bodies to make

181

the commitment. Finally I just said, "Do you think he'll jump." The passing strangers couldn't help themselves and finally looked up.

Two heads (or minds) are better than one

That may be true, unless they have been drinking, etc. or they are the boys depicted below.

Two boys are half a boy and three boys are no boys at all
*
When the going gets tough, the tough get going
*
MOST IRRITATING NOISE # 8

Many people possess the worthless ability to pop their gum while chewing. I find the noise very irritating. For some reason I cannot do this, but I don't see any actual need to be accomplished at it.

Simple things please little minds
*
Don't judge a man until you've been in his shoes
*
"All the people like us, are 'We' and everyone else is 'They'"
Rudyard Kipling
*
Different strokes for different folks
*
There's no fool like an old fool

First impressions are forever (last forever)

Changing someone's bad first impression of you is very hard to overcome. A person may not even know what others think of them. If you don't know there is a problem, you won't think to correct it. The best course of action is to make everyone's first impression of you be a positive one.

*

Everyone thinks himself able to advise others
*

Psychiatrist – Those who tell others how to manage their lives, when they may be seeking counsel themselves

I once had to visit a psychiatrist concerning Lynda's son, Brandon. He had begun to cause problems at home and in school. His attitude was rebellious and nonconforming. In other words, it stunk. The school counselor had set up the office appointment with the (no disrespect intended) shrink.

He asked me a few questions and I began to tell him about Brandon's offensive behavior at home. A few minutes into the story I witnessed a peculiar occurrence. He had fallen asleep. I knew I could be boring, but he was being paid to listen. I got up and quietly walked out. I never did hear from him. An apology would have been appropriate.

*

Give someone an inch and they will take a foot

Ray Racobs

*

It's like the blind leading the blind
*
You can't please everyone

We keep on trying though, don't we?
*
Clothes don't make the man (woman)
*
Keep up with the Joneses

I am thankful Lynda does not have the mind set like many who think they must have what others do and more.

*

Keep a thing for seven years and you will find a use for it

[Keep a thing for life and let your heirs deal with it.]

After my grandfather passed away, my mom took off work to spend time in Waco, Texas, with my Aunt Mary. They had the unenviable task of going through all of their father's personal effects. Their mother had passed on a few years previously, and they had already helped Granddaddy take care of those belongings, but this time the task was even more monumental.

Everything and the kitchen sink
I took a weeks vacation to drive down and assist in the cleanup of the house and grounds, so the

property could be sold. My grandfather had always been known to save things that he thought he could use at a later date. The amount of stuff we found in his work shop, outbuildings, garage, attic, and basement was unbelievable. I used the term "stuff", but that was being kind. It was junk and some of it was weird. He was a young man during the early '30's and had lived through the Great Depression.

The tough financial times of those years must have confused his sense of value. We found countless numbers of items that anyone else would just have thrown away, but he had saved. I will only mention two particular items as examples. I ran across a box whose contents were only small cotton balls. I thought that odd enough, but nearby were other boxes filled with nothing but empty Alka Seltzer bottles. He had evidently saved not only the bottles, but also the little cotton balls that came from the top of each bottle.

After all was said and done, we loaded, to the max, four of the largest trash dumpsters available with "treasures".

One man's trash is another man's treasure

*

A chip off the 'ole block

*

Many make mountains out of molehills

*

Everything is funny as long as it happens to

Ray Racobs

someone else
*

I think the next saying is cute for those of us who are experienced, with functioning brains.

There may be snow on the roof, but there is still a good fire in the stove below

Some of my "snow" must have melted.
It takes one to know one

I don't refer to females, women, ladies, or girls, as "guys". I seem to be in the minority against how the term "guys" is now used, but that is OK. I don't mind being correct over the majority of folks.

I was half-insulted when I first heard it said to me by a female server at a rather nice restaurant. I was taking my wonderful wife, Lynda, out for dinner, when we were asked, "What can I get you guys?" I told her, "My wife is not a guy." She did apologize, but Lynda reprimanded me after she had departed with our order, for making a big deal out of a common phrase used by all. "All", I told her, "does not include me." I strongly feel it is a poor form of speech and it illustrates how many of us have become lazy in our thought processes used before we speak. What was wrong with "Folks" or "You all"?

Not long after that incident, I happened to substitute a boys P.E. class at the local high school. I called a group of real guys "girls" during my directions to the class. They came unglued. After a

186

tense few moments, I explained, "If girls could be called guys, then it seems only right that guys could be called girls." They weren't buying it and I can't really blame them. It was not so acceptable when…..

The shoe was on the other foot
*

All people are good…
good for something or good for nothing
*

I'm from Missouri, show me
*

Optimist – One who looks on the bright or positive side of life…..The glass is half full

Pessimist – One who is, of course, not optimistic about life in general…..The glass is half empty
*

A chain is only as good as it's weakest link
*

I enjoy watching people and how they act in different circumstances. Take the time some day to watch a group of people standing in line for a show or a seat at a restaurant. I have noticed that men stand around and wait with their hands in their pockets, but women stand there and cross their arms on their chest. See if you observe the same actions.

Best laid plans of mice and men go awry.

PLANNING

This one has been referred to as the "5 P's".....

Prior Planning Prevents Poor Performance

I really feel there should be a few more <u>"P's"</u> in it.

[<u>Proper</u> Prior Planning <u>Probably</u> Prevents <u>Piss</u> Poor Performance]

*

It is a bad plan that can't be changed.

*

The best laid plans of mice and men go awry

*

Most of us spend some time planning prior to taking a trip. I am no different, but I put forth a lot of effort and time in my plans. I am not as detailed as I used to be, since I now try to plan any long trip down to the nearest hour instead of formulating an estimate down to the minute. It must be the perfectionist in me from being born a Leo. Oh all right, I will.....

Come clean and *Spill the beans*

It is Triple A Travel Service in Wichita who help me plan in that great of detail. Some of the services provided by AAA or other travel agencies are ones you don't particularly want to use, like towing. In a good plan you should anticipate for unpleasant happenings, because…..

Stuff happens
(A revised and more appropriate version of the words commonly used, but I wanted to keep this G rated.)
*

Preparations for our August 2000 migration or vacation, if you prefer, proceeded as usual. The pop up was loaded to the gills, as usual. We always take too much, I know, but I like to be prepared. The trip was routine. We were heading to Blue Mesa, as usual, but our stay there would be different. Lynda's sister and husband were going to meet us. They were driving up from Amarillo, Texas. I have always liked Brenda and John and the added company was sure to be a pleasure.

Lynda and I always take a day trip from the campground to hang out and shop at Crested Butte, north of Gunnison. Brenda and John wanted to go river rafting. On the route to our destination we drove through Almont, a small community whose main business is a float trip and rafting company. The decision was made to drop them off, proceed on to"Butte", and pick them up on our way back.

Things went as planned until we were ready to leave. The truck began to have a problem gaining any speed. My tachometer showed 3,000 rpm, but we were going at idle speed. I checked the fluid level, but it was fine. I found a small auto repair shop and described the problem to the mechanic. He said it was the transmission, but he couldn't help us. There was no major truck dealer in town. We were in trouble. It was time to call AAA.

The contact person was very efficient and helpful. She dispatched a tow truck, but there would be an inconvenient wait. Crested Butte is in an isolated part of Colorado. The woman did some checking and told of us about a shuttle bus service that operated between Crested Butte and Gunnison. She notified them and they agreed to swing by and pick Lynda up. I would remain behind with the truck.

I was to learn later that the driver drove by the river rafting location and picked up a surprised John and Brenda. The bus went on to Gunnison, but the camp was about fifteen miles farther. The driver agreed to take the stranded group on to Blue Mesa.

I traveled with the tow truck to the Dodge dealer in Gunnison, but they would not be able to work on it for a week. Another shop nearby would take the truck, so I rented a car and returned to Blue Mesa.

      The shop was able to replace the transmission just in time for us to return home before Lynda had to be back for school, but there were complications. The mechanic recommended that we not pull a trailer during the break-in period.

      We ended up making a deal with the manager of Blue Mesa. We traded the pop up camper to them in exchange for a week's cabin rental each summer for ten years. This deal didn't hurt Lynda's feelings at all, since she was tired of trailer camping.

      AAA made the stressful event more bearable and less costly. The transmission was only 197 miles over warranty, but Dodge eventually did agree to pay us for the part. If I had bought the extended warranty when I purchased the truck I would have saved money. I hadn't planned for the worst.

*

*

"A good plan today is better than a perfect plan tomorrow."

                                    Gen. George Patton

*

Shop 'till you drop.

SHOPPING

One of the biggest shopping days of the year
is said to be the day after Thanksgiving. I would have
to say that the vast majority of shoppers out that early
are women. That is quite understandable. Most guys
ate so much for dinner the day before they are lucky
to be alive, much less able to wake up that early.

What started out years ago to be a fun event
has now turned into large-scale mayhem that could
rival tag team wrestling. The evening news showed
footage about the day. It had tape of women fighting
in line. It showed many customers being run down in
store aisles, by other shoppers, after the store doors
were opened.

On the plains of Kansas, in the early morning
hours of late November, the temperature is not likely
to be very balmy. I am not, and never have been,
dumb enough or bored enough to get up in the wee
hours of the morning, just to stand in line for hours
to spend my money. Millions of people all across the
nation, in every town of any size, do just that.

I think the merchants should look at the whole
affair logically. They need to change how things are
done, so it will be safer for the public. There has to
be a better way to conduct a sale. If store owners do

not do something then local government should step in and legislate some kind of guidelines to follow.

"There are two chances of sending the wife shopping for one item and have her return with just that one item; slim and none."
Ray Racobs

*

Women seem to have more stamina than men do when it comes to shopping at the mall for hours. If shopping were picked as a new Olympic event, it would not be fair. I don't know how I can hike for a day and feel better than shopping for half a day.

*

Time flies when you're having fun.

SPORTS and GAMES

If you can't beat them, join them

[If you can't beat them, take them off your schedule.]
*

Golf – A game where one good shot out of a hundred will make you want to play again

I was about thirty when I played my first round of golf. I had hit golf balls before at driving ranges, but I had never been out on the links. I shot a 99, but I will always remember one particular shot of near excellence. It was about a 100 foot putt, on a long undulating green, with three or four breaks. I took a long hard look and assessed the situation. I hit the ball with firm confidence. It took a route that looked like it was following a snake. It ran up to the lip of the cup.....and stopped.

The three other guys of the foursome stood in disbelief. They wanted to wait to see if the wind or some other force of nature would somehow force the ball into the hole, but it just sat there. The affect of the shot gave me goose bumps and chills up my spine. I quickly forgot about the drives into other fairways, the unintentional drowning of two balls, and the missed putts from less than four feet.

*

Practice makes perfect

[Practice leads towards perfection]

A well known and popular professional golfer once said that the more he practiced the luckier he got.

*

Slow Pitch Softball – A ball game for those too old or too slow to play hard ball

*

I am not a hardcore sports "nut", who sits on the sofa for hours, through each weekend, watching the tube. Some "couch potatoes" view one sport or another, at length, every Saturday and Sunday of the year. Those sports fanatics with cable or satellite capabilities have the opportunity to follow a variety of sports every day or night of every calendar day. Here's some advice to anyone fitting the description presented in the previous sentence.

Get a life
*

My father would certainly have fit into that category if he were alive today. He passed away before all of the advances (if you consider them to be advances) in television. I have seen him watch two different sporting events on two TVs while having the radio tuned into another game. Was that a life? He would have loved split screen.

*

A winner never quits and a quitter never wins
Winning isn't everything, it's the only thing

198

*

Hockey – A game played on ice, where fighting often seems to be the main attraction and points scored are secondary, since there are so few anyway
*

It's not whether you win or lose that counts, it's how you played the game
*

Sportsmanship – Good conduct or character shown by those who participate in any area of competition

This is, unfortunately, almost non existent in many professional sports and has become a problem in some amateur athletic programs.
*

Nice guys finish last
*

Good things come in threes

is better than

Misfortunes never come singly
*

Fishing – The sport, which matches the intelligence of an angular with that of a fish…..Or…..An excuse to get out of the house

One Saturday afternoon, years ago, I went fishing with an older guy, who was a neighbor of mine. After we had packed up and said good-bye to the wives, we proceeded directly to the local grocery. I thought Bob needed to get some more beer, but he bought, instead, three nice sized catfish. Then we drove to a run-down club which, I knew, was Bob's favorite hangout. We never did go fishing, but sat at the bar and watched a baseball game on TV.

*

I have ***gone fishing*** a fair amount of time in the past, but haven't for probably a decade. I don't know why I quit fishing. At Camp Seikooc, there was a splendid pond where one could go to drown a few worms. I was fishing at the pond one day when Lynda drove up to chat. For some reason the topic of conversation ended up on my inability to give up the habit of smoking (always a touchy subject). I got so upset that I threw my fishing rod and reel into the pond. I haven't fished since.

Close only counts in horseshoes and hand grenades

One of my favorite outdoor games is that of horseshoes. At Blue Mesa the camp puts on a modest horseshoe tournament each Saturday. It is not a big affair and I usually win a free meal for taking first place. I had come to think that I was a good horse-shoe "thrower" until I ran across some really serious players at Oak Park CG near Colorado Springs. We visited the camp on the way home from Blue Mesa.

I entered their weekly tournament not thinking that I would soon be getting a lesson in "pitching" horseshoes. I managed to place fifth in the tournament, but I was humbled. I resigned to the fact that I was not that good. If I were to be competitive I

would have to practice. Lynda thought that being fifth
out of twenty was pretty good. She has, on occasion,
informed me that I am too competitive in several
areas. I don't disagree with her observation.

It's not that I mind not being great or the best
at something, but I don't want to be just average. I
strive to be at least very good at any endeavor. As
a kid I used to play chess, until I got beaten in three
(maybe four) moves. I never played again, because
I didn't care to learn the game better. I seem to have
been sidetracked or derailed, but that's all right.

I don't know why I became so competitive,
but it doesn't bother me. There is nothing wrong in
wanting to do well in what you do, but it doesn't just
happen. You must work to make it happen.

After returning home from vacation, I picked
up some "shoes" and practiced on my form and my
accuracy. Starwoods had two run down pits when we
first moved there. They were adequate enough for
what I wanted them for. I had a year to prepare. I
added Oak Park to our schedule for next summer.
We arrived on a Friday evening in time for
the tournament the next day. It would be, I hoped,
redemption time. It wasn't surprising that many of
those present at the event were familiar to me from
the previous August. Most of the full-time RV'ers
pull into the same campgrounds during the same time
period each year.

Charlie, the best player around was there. I heard that he had rarely been beaten and even does well in other bigger tournaments. The contest began and I was doing very well. My work at practicing had evidently paid off. Charlie and I had tied for the same number of wins and in points made. There would be a head to head competition between us.

It was quite an exciting affair. All of the other participants stood or sat around to watch and many of the campground guests had joined in for the spectacle. It was a little bit nerve wracking to be scrutinized by the crowd. If I were to choke......no, I could not think about it.

We had both gone over twenty points, but one had to be up by two to declare the winner. The match seemed to go in slow motion. Every toss was more than important, they were crucial. It was a thrilling game with an unbelievable ending. I threw first and hit a ringer....he countered with a ringer....My next throw didn't open up in time, but it was a "leaner". It was still only worth one point. I thought Charlie would try to knock my "pointer" away. If he missed I would win. He threw and my stomach knotted up. My leaner was still there, but he had thrown a ringer underneath it. He had won. I will hold very fond memories of that match forever. I was a happy loser.

*

Bingo – A boring game popular with senior citizens, which requires little more than just plain luck to win

I guess I never had enough cards to take up the slack time between the calling of the numbers.

*

Bing Hall – A smoke filled room where Bingo is played, of course.

Those who weren't sick when they came in may be by the time they leave.

*

Cheats never win and winners never cheat

I have played poker for money ever since being in the Navy. To me poker is no fun unless it is for money. When I used to drink, I usually lost. I owe it to my state of inebriation and not to bad luck. After I quit drinking, there was a period of several years that I never left the table a loser. I owe that to my knowledge of how to play the game. Being able to focus on the cards was helpful as well.

Before we moved to Starwoods, I would regularly play with the guys at the fire department. We would go to different homes and have a fun evening of nickel, dime, and quarter stakes. I was always a winner, until (as I found out later) the guys ganged up on me and I lost. Now, I won't go so far as to say they cheated, but in poker there are ways to play against another player and it would not be technically cheating, but I wouldn't say it was fair either.

*

Let the games begin

Not quite as exciting as "Gentlemen, start your engines", is it?

*

The ball's in your court

*

It's all over, but the shouting

*

Why is the crowd of spectators in tennis and golf matches required to keep quite while the players perform? On the other hand, the noise level in most other sports goes unchecked. Does a batter at the plate in baseball require less concentration to hit a ninety-five m.p.h. pitch compared to a tennis player receiving a serve from their opponent? I think not. The reason must stem from the country where the sport became popular. The British seem to be much more reserved than we are. Rugby would, of course, be an exception to the rule.

You can't get there until you leave.

TRAVEL

If you never leave, you will never get there

Take the road less traveled

Don't if it's a dirt road, after a good rain, without a 4-wheel drive vehicle.

*

Construction Zone – The best place for the police to set up a speed trap

*

You take the high road and I'll take the low road

*

Empty – What the gas gauge usually shows in a teenager's car

*

"He travels fastest, who travels alone."
Rudyard Kipling

STOP – What most drivers don't do at a stop sign

*

No trip is long with good company

When Lynda and I go somewhere together the travel time seems so much shorter. I know if you drive with someone and carry on a conversation it will seem as if the time went by faster, but what I feel is different. I am much more comfortable with Lynda beside me. The same holds true with.....

Time flies, when you're having fun

Anything boring seems to drag on and on, but when things are going good the time goes by too fast. The two weeks prior to our vacation departure date goes by like slow motion. Two weeks of the vacation is on fast forward.

*

Speed Limit – 5-15 miles per hour less than the speed of those driving

MOST IRRITATING NOISE # 9

It is my choice to listen to my car radio and decide what station and type of music to hear. Many motorists feel that everyone should hear what music they are playing on their radio. Sound at a very high decibel level is certainly not safe for one's hearing and they would never be able to hear an emergency vehicle's siren.

Close only counts in…

WAR

"War is hell."
General William Sheridan
*

Those three words say so much. There are those who relish war and conflict and that is too bad.
*

While I was stationed in Hawaii the war in Vietnam was escalating. I decided to volunteer for duty there instead of basking in the sun on Waikiki Beach. I put in for the battleship U.S.S. New Jersey or a River Patrol Boat squadron.

The New Jersey had been taken out of the "mothball" fleet to be refitted and was soon to be back on line. It would have been an honor to have been chosen as a member of the crew on the famous dreadnaught. I was not selected.

I did get orders for the Naval Air Station at Cam Rahn Bay, Republic of Vietnam. I was pleased to be going somewhere and I thought I could help in the "conflict". Anyway, Hawaii was too expensive.

While in Vietnam, I would receive overseas pay, hazardous duty pay, and at times combat pay on top of my base pay. All wages were also tax exempt. During my one-year tour and six-month extension, I would save enough money to buy a brand new car.

The weather at Cam Rahn was much the same as in Hawaii and they did have gorgeous beaches, but no bikinis. I actually went surfing and sailing while at CRB. The only excitement was going to the club after work.

My first tour was fairly uneventful and Cam Rahn was probably the safest place in Vietnam. Our squadron would fly support and logistics missions for the Army and Air Force. They were the ones directly involved with the conflict in the south. F-4 Fighters would take off from the air base side of the peninsula all day and all night, when the weather was good.

I extended my tour and was able to get a free week of R & R (rest and recuperation). I chose to go to Sidney, Australia. It was wonderful. The GI's who went there certainly boosted their economy. The city was beautiful, as were the women. We called them "round eyes", because we were so used to seeing "slant eyes". I don't mean to use the term for Asian women in a derogatory sense, but there were many who did and suppose still do. I think Oriental women are quite lovely.

Upon my return to CRB, I was surprised to find that I had received orders to report to Helicopter Attack (light) Squadron 3, or just HAL3 for short. My new duty station was located at Bien Thuy, RVN, which was in the delta to the south. I would finally be in the war. Our unit was the only one of its kind to see action in Vietnam for the Navy. Although my duties were of a non-combat nature, I often flew on logistic flights with the crews. On a few of these flights, we took "hits". I had the impression that the crew was elated to be able to respond to the threat by making rocket or strafing runs. The crew would receive more "points" towards air medals for flights involved with enemy action. The limited action I was involved in was exhilarating. The sound of the rotors mixed in with the report of the machine guns was exciting. I was qualified on the M-60, but never was able to use the "talent" as a door gunner.

I had probably been lucky not to have been selected to be on the PBR's, which was my other choice for Vietnam duty. They took a beating in the delta rivers and canals. I had the opportunity to visit one of their "bases". The accommodations I had at Cam Rahn would be like the Hilton Inn compared to how those souls lived. My tour with HAL-3 was not totally uncomfortable either.

While visiting the dock at a PBR camp I was shocked to see one of the boats that had not faired well in a recent "fire fight". The boat was "shot to hell". I learned that all crewmembers had been killed or severely wounded, which was not any surprise, after viewing the crippled vessel. To get a feeling of what those guys went through watch "Apocalypse Now" and probably double the intensity of the movie's fire fight scene.

HAL(3) lost several young officers, who had been pilots of the UH1B "Hueys", as well as "boys" who were the enlisted crewmen, but they became men, even if it were to be posthumously.

I was an E-5 at Cam Rahn Bay and had passed my E-6 test at HAL3. To accept the higher grade level advancement I would have had to extend my enlistment for another two years, but I was done and wanted to go home.

*

If one lives by the sword, he will die by the sword
*

My father spent much of his time in the Army (Army/Air Corps back then) after Pearl Harbor in security or Military Police. He never would tell me "war stories" and I never asked. Was I interested? Yes, I was, but until my adult years, I was actually afraid of him or at least not comfortable to be in his presence.

*

Since I experienced the feeling of war, I can see why he didn't want to talk about it. I wasn't shot at often, but it only takes once to be a statistic. I was proud to serve in Vietnam in a cause that I believed in. It is a shame that others didn't feel the same way. The effort there was often thwarted by politics. We accomplished nothing in Vietnam, partly due to the public protests. Those who fought and died there are still heroes in my book and I respect all Vietnam vets.

"We are not retreating; we are advancing in

another direction."
General Douglas MacArthur
*

Every man for himself
*

"I have not yet begun to fight."
John Paul Jones
*

We have faced the enemy and they are us.

[We have faced the enemy and we don't know who the heck they are]
*

"Give me liberty or give me death."
Patrick Henry
*

"I regret that I have but one life to give to my country."
Ethan Allen

I don't remember the exact quote, but General George Patton said something to the effect that …..
The idea is not to die for ones country, but to make the other "bastard" die for his. I've always admired Patton, because he spoke what was on his mind.
*

War makes thieves and peace hangs them
*

"Damn the torpedoes! Full speed ahead."
Admiral Farragut

"A house divided against itself cannot stand."
Abraham Lincoln

"There never was a good war or a bad peace."
Benjamin Franklin

Now, I have to take exception to that quote, if in fact 'ole Ben really said it. If a peace wasn't bad, we would probably still be singing "God save the Queen" instead of the "Star Spangled Banner". I wonder how many third world countries feel that peace isn't bad. I heartily agree that war is never good, but at times, it may be necessary.

*

"No nation ever had an army large enough to guarantee it against attack in time of peace or ensure it victory in time of war."
Calvin Coolidge

*

"This was not an act of terrorism; it was an act of war."
George W. Bush

*

Don't give up the ship

*

Shoot now and ask questions later

*

Stand up and be counted

*

I have read much, over the years, about the Civil War. President Abraham Lincoln was given the results of a battle that had taken the lives of many generals, thousands of troops, and even hundreds of the cavalry's horses. He remarked that he had plenty of generals to spare, but he didn't have enough horses to lose.

*

Soldiers in peacetime are like chimneys in summer
*

All quiet on the Western front
*

Divide and conquer
*

An army marches on it's stomach
*

All's fair in love and war
*

Anything goes
*

No holds barred
*

Raining cats and dogs.

WEATHER

Many sayings about the weather have come from the experiences of those brave (or crazy) souls who crossed the vast oceans and seas to explore the unknown.

I have imagined myself on the Mayflower, in 1620, with the folks who left England and headed for "New England" to start a new life. My first words after loosing sight of land, would probably have been, "Oh, manure", or something to that effect. By the way, over half of them died before they saw the next spring.

Red sky in the morning is a sailor's sure warning
When it rains, it pours
*

When the rooster crows at night, he will wake with a
wet head
*

Weather – What everyone talks about when they have nothing else to say

Weather Forecasters – Those who get paid, even when they are wrong

*

Wind in the east 'tis neither good for man nor beast
*

The sharper the storm, the sooner it's over
*

Umbrella – Something one never has when they need it

*

Rain before seven, fine before eleven.
*

A rooster will wake with a wet head if he crows at night

    I used to have a bunch of roosters and they were lucky not to be shot for crowing at night. The idea that they only crow at sunrise is false.

*

The darkest hour comes before the storm
*

Too close for comfort

    Kansas is in "Tornado Alley", as much of the Midwest is often called. It didn't get to share the name, with other states, just by chance. Every year, usually in the springtime, our area around Wichita, experiences numerous tornado warnings (actual sightings) and watches (possible tornados).

*

In the spring of 1991, on April 26th, an "F-5" tornado began a path of death and destruction from the area of Clearwater, KS, near where I live now, and traveled northeast through Andover, KS, where I lived then. When the area sirens went off I had three groups of Girl Scouts staying at the camp. Camp Seikooc was only a mile east of town. The tornado shelters at the cabin sites were 5' tall, round, concrete culvert pipes, which were laid end to end and covered with dirt.

The only basement on camp was at the main lodge, where one group went for shelter. I was out in front of the lodge watching the direction of the huge, massive cloud of debris, until several full-sized 4x8' sheets of plywood went sailing over my head. I then joined the girls in the basement, but after a short time I could no longer hear the howling wind. We all went upstairs and outside. It was surprisingly a gorgeous and calm evening. It was 6:40 p.m.

Everyone at the two cabin sites were all right. There was tree damage everywhere. My old shop had sustained the most structural damage of any of the buildings on site. It looked like someone had picked it up, turned it upside down, and threw it back to the ground again. The tornado's devastating path had come within 300 feet of where one of the troops was sheltered. They were very lucky.

There were fifteen people who weren't as lucky. Two lost their lives in Wichita and thirteen died in Andover, eleven of which were in the trailer court less than a mile from the camp. Most of them had made a bad decision to ride out the tornado in their homes, rather than seek better shelter. Over 350 homes and many businesses were destroyed.

The infamous tornado had traveled seventy miles on the ground in about an hour's time, which shows how fast they can move. The "F" in F-5 stands for "Force". An F-6 is really a rarity. Only 2% of the tornados reported are F-5, which pack winds up to 250 mph.

Kansas ranks third, behind Texas and then Oklahoma, among all the states, for the frequency of tornados. I was in the fifth grade when we moved to Kansas from Texas in 1957. My mother was always paranoid of them, since she was raised in Texas and was familiar with their devastation.

Every time tornado warnings were issued, we kids were ordered to the bathroom. The smallest room in a house, without a basement, is supposed to be the safest place to be, but with a direct hit it does not matter. In that event, you had better say a prayer and kiss your butt goodbye. I don't ever remember being afraid of the threat of tornados and must have become familiar with our "tornado shelter", since I would simply fall asleep in the bathtub. I don't recall where my mom would go. My dad was always called back to the air base, since he was in charge of flight line security.

*

Mobile Home Park – Tornado magnet

*

I would never seek shelter in a house without a basement. I would prefer to drive away from the area. Fortunately, Starwoods has five shelters on site. Three of them have been constructed to withstand the force of an F-5.

*

Did you know that Mount Washington, NH, has the distinction of having the highest recorded wind speed at 231 mph? That must be for straight line winds, since tornadoes produce higher speeds.

Any port in the storm
*

Red sky at night is the sailor's delight

No weather is ill if the wind be still

Ray Racobs

April showers bring May flowers
*

So we began with the Mayflower and end with the May flowers.

Don't put off…

YOU CAN DO IT

Easy as 1, 2, 3

One step at a time

I am often asked to put something together. I hate those dreaded words on the outside of any box; "Some assembly required". I know, from experience in the past, there will be frustration, anger, and more time involved than the word "some" would indicate.

Keep in mind.....

It's always easier said than done
*
It's a piece of cake

The product which needs to be assembled was, more likely than not, made in a foreign country. China, Japan, and Mexico are just a few of the many countries, who export to the United States. Yes, there are always directions, of some sort, enclosed to guide one through the assembly process. They often seem to be lacking the proper translation for me to fully understand what they want me to do. After completing the process I invariably find a few parts lying on the floor. If a company sends more parts

than what are needed, I wish they would tell me so.
I quit spending more time trying to figure out where
the other little nuts and bolts may go. If the finished
product doesn't fall apart, I throw them away.

Easy as pie

Sometimes a product will not need to be
assembled, but other frightening words may be
present on the packaging. When your gift or purchase
requires installation you are not going to have a good
day.

*

Too many irons in the fire

I often try to do too many things at one
time for the sake of time management....or at least
that is what I tell myself. The idea is good in theory
and is practical in some situations. At other times
I.....

Run around like a chicken with its head cut off

Or like how my one legged duck swam....in circles.
*
There's always a first time for everything
*
You never know what you can do until you try
*
Like taking candy from a baby
*
Take it easy

Been there, done that

A tee shirt is usually purchased to prove it.
*

Don't start what you can't finish
*

Go for it
*

Close, but no cigar
*

All systems go
*

Don't bite off more than you can chew
*

MOST IRRITATING NOISE # 10

The last on my abbreviated list of irritating noises is a dripping faucet, but if I have to put up with the noise, it is my own fault for not fixing the darn thing. I **can do it**, but I often procrastinate. At times, I can't find one of those "round tuits". They can be awfully illusive.

*****GRIZZLY'S FAVORITES *****

Hope for the best, but prepare for the worst

I try to keep a version of that one in mind when things are not going well for me. It is…..

[Hope for the best, expect the worst and anything in between will be all right.]

To illustrate this consider…..

He who expects nothing will never be disappointed

and

Something is better than nothing
*
To stay on track and keep things in perspective it also helps me to focus on…..

The Serenity Prayer

God,
Grant me the serenity to accept
the things I cannot change, the
courage to change the things I can,
and the wisdom to know the difference.
Do unto others as you would have them do unto
you

227

If everyone in the world would buy into that saying, just think how wonderful everything could be. It is often the simplest words that project the most powerful meanings. It is such a shame that there are so many evil, self centered, hypocritical people in our midst today and yesterday. The past is part of the problem. There are races of people who have been battling each other for centuries and for what? Because their ancestors did it and they want to get even, but no one will ever be even.

What will it take to bring about true world peace? Some might say that more religion is needed. It certainly wouldn't hurt, but I doubt it. There have probably been as many people killed for the sake of religion than for any other reason. I know what it will take. All of the bad and evil people need to be removed from this world. Will it ever happen? That's a good question.

*

"If anything can go wrong, it will go wrong."
Murphy's Law

*

EPILOGUE

All's well that ends well
*

My project is done and will be shipped off to 1st Books soon for publishing. Lynda is still fretting with her 24 page children's book, *Cricketta Noel.* I have almost completed <u>Oro, The Incredible Dog</u>. I have also worked on writing several fictional short stories for a future book. I guess …..

That will remain to be seen
*
All good things must come to an end

I said "good" things ….. not great, but

I truly hope you enjoyed most of *Grizzly's This 'N That.* I have enjoyed writing most of it, so maybe it evens out somewhere along the way.
*
The rest is history
*

About the Author

Physically Ray Racobs is a resident of Kansas, but mentally, as "Grizzly", he lives in the mountains of Colorado. Grizzly's This'N That is his first completed book-length literary endeavor.

Over the years, he has written various articles, commentaries, and editorials for several Wichita area newspapers and organizational newsletters. He has been working on a collection of short stories and tales for another book.

Ray has been a Girl Scout Camp Ranger for over twenty-three years. He was the 2003 "Friend of the Year" for the Haysville Community Library and is a staff writer for the Haysville Times. Since 1997, Ray's greatest joy away from work has been his role as a substitute teacher in neighboring school districts.